THE ROAD TO SUSTAINABILITY IN THE UK AND GERMAN BIOTECHNOLOGY INDUSTRIES

Dr Hannan E. Kettler,
Office of Health Economics, London
and Dr Steven Casper, *Wissenschaftszentrum
für Sozialforschung, Berlin*

Office of Health Economics
12 Whitehall London SW1A 2DY

2

© July 2000, Office of Health Economics, Price £10.00
ISBN 1 899040 61 7
Printed by BSC Print Ltd., London

Acknowledgements

We would like to acknowledge the many people who contributed their time, views, and documentation. A list is provided at the end of the report. A special thank you goes to Tessa Westbrook for all the time and energy she put into editing drafts, tracking data, and updating the tables.

Our research was partly financed by a Targeted Social-Economic Research Grant under the Third Research and Technological Framework Programme of the European Commission. The results will contribute to a Research Project entitled: Sectoral Systems in Europe: Innovation, Competitiveness, and Growth which is sponsored by this grant. We would also like to thank participants from the ESSY group for their comments on earlier drafts.

About the authors

Dr Hannah Kettler is a research economist at the Office of Health Economics, specialising in the pharmaceutical industry. She has published several books and articles on the economics of the pharmaceutical research and development process.

Dr Steven Casper is a Senior Research Fellow at the Wissenschaftszentrum Berlin and, starting in autumn 2000, will be a Lecturer in Entepreneurship and Innovation at the Judge Institute of Management Studies, University of Cambridge. His research focuses on institutional determinants of innovation processes in high-technology industries.

OFFICE OF HEALTH ECONOMICS

4   Professor Lord Maurice Peston – *Professor of Economics, Queen Mary and Westfield College*
Professor Carol Propper – *Department of Economics, University of Bristol*
Mr Nicholas Wells – *Head of European Outcomes Research, Pfizer Ltd*
Professor Peter Zweifel – *Socioeconomic Institute, University of Zurich*

CONTENTS

List of Tables   6

List of Figures   6

Executive Summary   9

1 Introduction   13

2 Industry performance and structure in Germany
   and the UK   18

3 The dynamics of the biotechnology industry   29
   3.1 High risks and costs   30
   3.2 Innovation over a network   36
   3.3 Demand for biotechnology products – relationships
        with pharmaceutical companies   40
   3.4 An industry changing over time   45
   3.5 Summary   48

4 The national institutions approach and the case of
   technology transfer   50
   4.1 Introduction to the national institutions approach   50
   4.2 Technology transfer – the issue   51
   4.3 Technology transfer in Germany   53
   4.4 Technology transfer in the UK   58

5 Finance   63
   5.1 Financing biotechnology – the issue   63
   5.2 Financial markets in Germany   66
   5.3 Financial markets in the UK   75

6 Labour markets for scientists and managers   86
   6.1 Staffing companies – the issue   86
   6.2 Labour market structures in Germany   90
   6.3 Labour market structures in the UK   95

7 Conclusion and policy implications   99

References   105
Appendix 1 – Exchange rate table   114
Appendix 2 – Contributors   115

6 List of Tables

2.1 State of the biotechnology industry, 1998   18
2.2 Leading public biotechnology companies in the US and
     Europe   20
2.3 Products in the pipelines of European public biotechnology
     companies, 1999   21
2.4 Biotechnology business models   25
3.1 Toolbox companies' performance   47
4.1 Biotechnology SMEs in Germany   57
5.1 Biotechnology IPOs on the Neuer Markt in 1999   68
5.2 Seed-finance in the Munich BioRegio   70
5.3 Genome Pharmaceuticals Corporation seed- and start-up
     financing   70
5.4 UK and US venture capital investment by industry,
     1994-1998   82

List of Figures

2.1 New biotechnology firm creation in Germany, 1980-1999   22
2.2 The size structure of German biotechnology and UK
     biopharmaceutical companies, 1998   23
2.3 The age profile of German biotechnology and UK
     biopharmaceutical companies, 1998   24
2.4 UK biopharmaceutical strategy structure, 1994 and 1996   26
2.5 Product structures in Germany (1998) and the UK (1999)   27
2.6 Main business activities in German biotechnology
     companies   28
3.1 Biopharmaceutical products in development, world wide   32
3.2 Biotechnology-based products and other NMEs launched
     world wide, 1990-1999   33
3.3 Biotechnology products and other NMEs launched
     1992-1998, by therapeutic class   34
3.4 Types of companies originating and marketing biotechnology
     products world wide, 1982-1998   35
3.5 Biopharmaceutical products in development by therapeutic
     class, 1998   36

3.6   Biotechnology products in research and on the market by
      therapeutic class, 1998   37
3.7   The bioscience growth cycle   38
3.8   Providers of finance over the biotechnology firm lifecycle   39
3.9a Number of pharmaceutical alliances   40
3.9b Total dollar volume of pharmaceutical alliances   41
3.10 Alliances between the top 20 pharmaceutical companies and
      biotechnology firms   44
4.1   Location of biotechnology companies in Germany   56
4.2   Biotechnology 'clusters' in the UK   61
5.1   American Stock Exchange Biotechnology Index (BTK),
      October 1989 – July 1998   65
5.2   German 'public venture capital' of the tbg by sector,
      1996-1999   69
5.3   New venture capital investments in the UK and Germany,
      all sectors   72
5.4   Venture capital investments in the biotechnology industry,
      1994-1998   73
5.5   Biotechnology investment as a proportion of total venture
      capital, 1994-1998   74
5.6   Venture capital investment by stage, 1998   78
5.7   UK venture capital investment by stage, 1984 and 1998   79
5.8a US venture capital investment by stage, 1992-1998   80
5.8b UK venture capital investment by stage, 1992-1998   81
5.9   Relative performance of continental European, UK and US
      biotechnology stock indexes, August 1996-July 1998   84

8

EXECUTIVE SUMMARY

The UK and Germany are Europe's leaders in biotechnology with the most companies, employees and greatest sums invested in biotechnology research and development (R&D). The two countries' biotechnology sectors display important differences, however. Also, both remain well behind the US, the global leader in terms of number, size, maturity and profitability of companies.

This report examines the nature and origin of the differences between the biotechnology industries in the UK and Germany. We find that the differences in growth trajectories, choice of business models and sub-sector areas of specialization between the UK and Germany are linked to their different national institutions. The relevant national institutions are those that support competency building in the areas of technology transfer (i.e. commercialisation), finance and staffing.

While countries can learn from each other's experiences, where industries are at different growth stages and are surrounded by dissimilar institutional structures, as with biotechnology in the UK and Germany, different national policies will be appropriate in each case.

The biotechnology start-up dynamic in Germany took off almost ten years later than in the UK. At the end of 1998, half of German firms were no more than five years old and 45 percent had ten or fewer employees. In addition to being smaller and younger, German companies have focused on different product sub-sectors than UK companies: over 60 percent of German biotechnology companies operate in platform technology, service and diagnostic areas and only 16 percent are in therapeutics. As of 1999, none of the five public German biotechnology companies had therapeutic products in clinical trials.

The UK, by contrast, has a more mature industry, with a broader range of company sizes, ages and business model categories than in Germany. In 1998, more than 80 percent of UK biopharmaceutical firms had existed for six years or more, and over 40 percent had more than 100 employees. A third of UK biopharmaceutical companies seek to develop therapeutics. As of the end of 1999, the 43 public UK biotechnology companies, as a group, had an estimated 75 medicines in human clinical trials. Only one UK biotechnology company has successfully launched a new medicine onto the market, however, and

10 none of the top companies, ranked by market capitalisation, are yet earning profits.

The risks and costs of bringing new products to market are large. On average it takes 11 years and hundreds of millions of Euros to bring a targeted compound through clinical trials to market. Eighty-two percent of projects that enter clinical trials are terminated before completion. To operate in this uncertain environment, companies look to collaborate with other actors in the R&D network: pharmaceutical companies, other biotechnology companies, universities, and contract research organisations. To innovate and grow, companies must develop competencies to commercialise new technologies, to access external sources of finance, and to recruit and retain capable and experienced research scientists and managers.

The date of entry into an industry affects a company's choice of competitive strategy and market segment. Thus changes over time in technology, and in the expectations and priorities of finance providers, might be expected to have generated different profiles and trajectories for the biotechnology industries in Germany – developed in the mid 1990s – and the UK – established a decade earlier. However, we argue that the stronger source of differences between the UK and German industries is the difference between the two countries' respective national institutions that support technology transfer, finance and labour markets for scientists and managers.

Germany's financial institutions and its laws governing genetic engineering, intellectual property, and employment created long-standing institutional obstacles to the development of high-technology industries and markets for venture capital and entrepreneurial scientists. In the second half of the 1990s, however, the Federal German government took steps to remove some of the obstacles, thereby spurring the development of the biotechnology industry. Policies have been concentrated on providing start-up capital and on orchestrating linkages between university research and technology transfer centres, venture capitalists, and new start-ups. Regional support infrastructures have also been developed such as incubator laboratories, training and recruitment of local experts in patent law, and provision of business development planning and other services. Public money and lower-risk bank finance have backed many of the start-up projects. To secure future funds under such conditions, companies have tended to pursue platform technology strategies that are perhaps less risky and certainly take less time to develop and market than new therapeutics.

From the standpoint of labour, norms which deter quick hires and fires, and poor incentives for risk-taking career moves, make it difficult for German firms to change research trajectories quickly, for example, by closing down some facilities altogether. This, combined with the generally tight German labour markets for experienced managers and technicians in biotechnology, has also contributed to firms choosing the platform technology area. In addition to the lower financial risks involved, if core technologies in this area are more stable, long-term human resource commitments should be easier to sustain.

Using the US as a basis for comparison, the UK has developed broadly similar institutions to support high-risk, therapeutics-dominated corporate strategies. On that basis it has developed Europe's first and largest biotechnology industry. However, over the past couple of years, the industry has stalled and a critical mass of successful UK biotechnology companies has not yet developed. Clinical trials for some leading products have produced disappointing results and key companies have had problems recruiting and keeping experienced managers. Capital markets have responded positively to recent mergers and news about product developments but new companies continue to report difficulties securing sufficient venture capital to bridge the gap between the early start-up stage and an initial public offering of shares (IPO).

Our research points to a number of weaknesses in the UK incentive network. Key shortages of both finance and expertise appear to exist within university technology transfer offices. While a vibrant venture capital community with access to mature capital markets exists, in recent years the bulk of venture capital has been channelled into less risky investments promising quicker returns, such as management buy-ins/buy-outs rather than early stage investments. Finally, although UK labour markets are largely deregulated and firms can deploy the high-powered incentive structures needed to compete in innovation, there nevertheless appear to be shortages of talented scientists and managers willing to work within promising UK biotechnology firms. As with venture capital, risk aversion could be a factor; top UK researchers relocating to the US could be another.

In the medium-term, German and UK policy makers face different issues. German policy needs to become more diffuse to respond to the increasingly diversified needs of growing companies in a range of product segments. Until now, the German government has focused on the start-up stage and has made sector-specific exemptions to employment and tax laws so as to allow companies to become established. In the future, wider institutional and regulatory reforms may be required for the industry to flourish. In the UK, supply-related factors need to be addressed, especially in making available finance for the stages between start-up and IPO, improving the supply of skilled managers, and increasing resources for the technology transfer offices. In our view, current UK focus on 'coordination problems' addressed by cluster policies, must be complemented by attention to these technology transfer, finance and labour supply issues.

1 INTRODUCTION

Huge sums are invested annually in biotechnology[1] and yet there are few biotechnology-based therapeutics on the market to show for these huge up-front investments. But despite the low productivity so far, public and private scientists and businesses see great potential returns from biotechnology in the long run for the health and pharmaceutical industries. In the shorter term, governments also expect sizeable economic benefits from this innovation-driven industry. The US is the clear leader in the creation of small, entrepreneurial biotechnology firms. Driven to catch up with this world leader, European governments strive to design policies to improve the competitive performance of their biotechnology industries.

This paper examines the complex set of international marketplace dynamics, national market rules and regulations, and policies that, together, create the environment within which entrepreneurs, scientists, and financiers develop biotechnology start-up companies. We focus on the cases of the UK and Germany. These countries are the European leaders in biotechnology in terms of number of companies, employment, and investment. This accomplishment is attributed to the strength of each country's biomedical research base as well as the existence of strong, internationally competitive, domestic pharmaceutical industries plus governmental support in terms of financial assistance and mentoring at the start-up stage. Nonetheless, the UK and Germany exhibit different development paths and strategic profiles and both have yet to create a critical mass of viable biotechnology companies.

To explain these country differences and problems, we focus our analysis on the competencies that small technology firms need to successfully develop. The types of competencies needed are shaped by international factors, especially in the marketing of products and the formation of alliances between large pharmaceutical corporations and

---

1 In this paper, we concentrate on the strategies, constraints and successes of dedicated companies in the pharmaceutical and related technology and diagnostic segments of the biotechnology industry. Most data sources, however, do not distinguish between different industry segments. Unless otherwise specified, the figures in the tables cover the entire industry including the agro-bio and environment segments of biotechnology.

14   biotechnology firms. However, firms' access to, or ability to develop, the key resources and relationships are strongly influenced by national and local environments.

We identify critical 'competencies' for company development: incentives for universities and public research laboratories to commercialise technology; access to high-risk private and public finance; staff with skills in the relevant science areas, and; experienced managers. The orientations of the institutions that support these areas differ markedly between the UK and Germany.

Though on a much smaller scale, the UK biotechnology industry has developed within a regulatory context and pattern of market organisation similar to that in the US. However, while the UK has fostered many promising biotechnology firms over the last 15 years, its industry has yet to launch a blockbuster[2] along the lines of Amgen's Epogen. In 1998 and 1999 high profile setbacks among some of the UK industry's most prominent biotechnology firms shook confidence within financial circles and raised questions about whether the UK had companies with the compounds and development capabilities to achieve the success inferred in their valuations. Despite the rebound of share prices in late 1999 and early 2000, questions about the fundamental value of the UK industry remain. In response, the UK government is considering new policies to better support biotechnology firms, especially within the context of local university-based cluster arrangements (DTI, 1999; Sainsbury et al., 1999). An important question is whether these efforts are correctly targeted and adequately financed.

The development of a dedicated German biotechnology industry throughout the 1980s and early 1990s was thwarted by a number of industry-specific regulatory barriers against genetic engineering laboratory practices as well as by the absence of institutions, especially in the area of finance, needed to support start-ups in high-risk technology sectors. The liberalisation of some of these barriers in 1993 plus the introduction of sector specific technology policies has spurred the cre-

---

2 A blockbuster's annual sales exceed $500 million.

ation of dedicated German biotechnology companies. By some accounts, more than 400 such firms exist in total, several dozen of them in the health care segment. Most of these firms are still in their early growth stages and are far from bringing products to market, but commentators are linking the rapid growth of German biotechnology to governmental policy (see Adelberger, forthcoming; Ernst & Young, 1999). Though still far behind the UK in terms of employment and overall investment in biotechnology, Germany is now perceived as a serious threat to the UK's lead in Europe (DTI, 1999).

These recent developments – the growth spurt of start-ups in Germany and the disappointing performance of some of the leading biotechnology firms in the UK in 1998 and 1999 – call into question somewhat stereotypical conceptions of the relative ability of these two economies to successfully promote high-technology industries such as biotechnology.

The 'varieties of capitalism literature' links national institutional arrangements to a country's ability to compete successfully in specific activities. It suggests that companies in high risk, knowledge-based industries such as biotechnology would perform better in 'deregulated' systems such as those in the US and UK than in 'co-ordinated' economies such as Germany. Our micro-level analyses of the industries in the UK and Germany allow us to provide a sophisticated model of the links between institutions and performance in this sector. National institutional arrangements do play a pivotal role in the companies' growth trajectories and strategic choices. However, there may be more than one way to grow and succeed in this industry where different types of institutional arrangements support the different strategic options.

These findings contribute to the current policy debates, especially in the UK where policy makers seek to understand why German technology policies have been so successful and wonder aloud whether these policies would make sense in the UK context. Our analysis suggests that there is no 'one policy fits all'. Institutional differences limit the transfer of policies across borders.

This paper is organised into five sections followed by a conclusion. The general approach of the paper is to combine an analysis of industry dynamics and firm-level strategy with a discussion of national institutional variables.

Section 2 describes the performance and structure of the UK and German biotechnology industries. Despite their existence within a common global industry context, the UK and German industries have evolved differently with different product and growth strategies. We examine the global dynamics of the industry and the competencies that companies need to succeed in order to try and understand these differences.

Section 3 focuses on the global industry dynamics. Biotechnology companies operate in a complex network involving universities, research institutes, venture capitalists, service providers, regulators, and large pharmaceutical companies. The constellation of actors changes over the companies' growth phases. Furthermore, these growth phases (and networks) are different for different product strategies.

Sections 4, 5, and 6 investigate the operating conditions for biotechnology companies in the UK and Germany. In particular we look at the technology transfer nexus, the financial markets and the labour markets for skilled scientists and managers. For each of these areas we describe the general competency-related problems facing firms, relying on the US as the base case example, and then examine how domestic institutional environments and policies influence strategies available for firms in each country. We suggest that key institutional arrangements across countries strongly impact the structure of each country's biotechnology sector, and can thus help to explain why the UK and German industries have evolved in different directions.

In the concluding section (Section 7), we discuss the implications of our analysis for government policy. Most broadly, we suggest that policy may play an important role in shaping the resources and incentives facing firms, but must work through long-standing institutional arrangements. We find that a large number of current German policies are designed to fundamentally create or, in some cases, supplement technology transfer, corporate governance rules, and financial institutions. By contrast, in the UK a set of enabling institutions exists but seems to be relatively poorly organised to address the broader range and quality of problems faced by UK companies. To deal with these **17** issues, policies different from those used in Germany are required. Rather than create basic institutions from scratch, the UK government needs to fine-tune and better finance existing institutions and policies.

The arguments developed here derive from two core sources. The prime source is field research conducted by the authors in the UK and Germany during the first half of 1999. Over a six-month period we conducted interviews with managers at biotechnology firms in each country, as well as with venture capitalists, investment bankers, technology transfer officials at universities and public agencies, and officials at government agencies. The list of people interviewed is found in Appendix 1. Secondly, these qualitative field research results are supplemented in the paper by a number of industry analyses, such as the annual surveys produced by Ernst & Young and Arthur Andersen, as well as by other studies available from the academic literature.

2 INDUSTRY PERFORMANCE AND STRUCTURE IN GERMANY AND THE UK

This section provides an overview of the current structure of the German and UK biotechnology sectors[3]. Where possible, the US is used as a base for comparison. We highlight three areas in which important cross-country differences exist: 1. industry size, measured in terms of employment and number of firms; 2. industry maturity, measured in terms of age profile of companies, profitability, and the number of products on the market; and 3. sub-sector composition. The US industry is the largest and most mature of the three, with the UK running in second. When looking at the German and UK cases specifically, we find that the majority of German companies are smaller and younger and specialise in platform technologies. The UK sub-sector profile is more varied, with a sizeable share of their public companies developing therapeutics as well as technologies.

Table 2.1 **State of the biotechnology industry, 1998**

	US	Europe	UK	Germany
Number of companies	1,283	1,178	275	225
Number of public companies (1999)	327	68	43	5
Number of employees	153,000	45,823	15,854	4,013
Revenues ($\in$[4] million)	15,777	3,709	2,203	293
R&D expenditure ($\in$ million)	8,398	2,334	449	143
Net loss ($\in$ million)	4,326	2,107	n/a	35

Notes: The financial figures are for public companies only.
UK employment figure is for 1999. The BIA (1999a) put the estimate at 35,000-40,000, a figure that must include service and consulting companies as well as research facilities.
n/a = Not available.
Sources: Arthur Andersen (2000); Ernst & Young (1998a, 1999); Schitag Ernst & Young (1998).

3 The data presented in this section include all product segments of the biotechnology industry, and not just biopharmaceuticals, unless otherwise specified.
4 The Euro ($\in$) became an official common European currency for member countries on January 1, 1999 when one Ecu = one Euro ($\in$). We will use the term Euro ($\in$) to represent Ecu throughout the paper.

Table 2.1 compares the key indicators of industry structure for the **19** US, UK and Germany. Table 2.2 provides information about the largest public biotechnology companies in the three countries.

The US biotechnology industry is the world's largest, seen clearly by the number of companies and employees in Table 2.1. It is also the only country with a significant number of profitable biotechnology companies. According to Burrill and Company (1999), 12 of the 13 top US companies with market capitalisation exceeding $2 billion earned profits in 1998. Ten of these 13 are therapeutics companies, two are drug delivery companies and one, Sepracor, produces enabling technologies[5]. There were also a handful of profitable companies in the second tier of public biotechnology companies (those with market capitalisations between $500 million and $2 billion) (ibid., 127). It is important to point out, however, that the majority of US companies are loss makers. According to Warburg Dillon Read (2000b, 5), 'of the c300 publicly quoted companies in the US, c10 percent are profitable or close to profitability'. SG Cowen (2000a, 4) confirms this view – '307 of the 327 public US biotechnology companies continue to burn cash'.

The profiles of the top UK and German companies relative to the top US companies are very different. In addition to being many times larger, the US companies are almost all therapeutics companies (five of the top seven). These drug producers have products on the market, and, with the exception of MedImmune, are earning profits. So far only two UK biotechnology drugs have gained market approval: Celltech's (since its merger with Chiroscience) Chirocaine was approved in 1999 and is now on the UK market. The same company's Mylotarg received FDA approval in the US in May 2000 and is likely to be approved in Europe later in 2000 but at the time of writing (end-May 2000) was not yet available on the market. As of May 2000, none of the therapeutics research companies in the top group were earning profits. All the public companies in Germany are technology producers.

---

5 Sepracor was the only company in the group earning a loss in 1998.

20

Table 2.2 **Leading public biotechnology companies in the US and Europe**

Biotechnology company	Exchange	Commercial strategy	Marketed medicines	Products in development	Market capitalisation May 2000 (€ mill)	Revenues 1998 (€ mill)	Pre-tax profit/loss 1998 (€ mill)	R&D costs 1998 (€ mill)	Employees	Date founded	Date listed
UK/Germany											
Axis-Shield plc	LSE/Oslo	Technology platforms	N/A	N/A	176.25	10.56*	−10.08*	2.68*	225	1982	1999
Celltech Group plc	LSE	Therapeutics	1**	20	2,973.36	16.75	−4.44	15.02	574	1980	1993
Evotec Biosystems GmbH	Neuer Markt	Technology platforms	N/A	N/A	960.37	7.28	−8.25	8.25	215	1993	1999
MorphoSys AG	Neuer Markt	Technology platforms	N/A	N/A	626.09	4.55	−0.63	3.97	85	1992	1999
Oxford GlycoSciences plc	LSE	Hybrid	0	1	658.61	7.31	−12.43	18.94	113	1998	1998
PowderJect Pharmaceuticals plc	LSE	Hybrid	0	4	402.65	4.47	−6.74	10.46	124	1993	1997
Qiagen N.V	Neuer Markt	Technology platforms	N/A	N/A	3,112.59	94.02	15.08	10.95	925	1985	1996
US											
Amgen Inc.	NASDAQ	Therapeutics	3	11	37,993.17	2,317.91	735.11	538.12	5,500	1980	1983
Biogen Inc.	NASDAQ	Therapeutics	4	10	9,209.54	475.86	161.18	124.51	1,400	1978	1983
Celera Genomics	NYSE	Technology platforms	N/A	N/A	5,970.96	3.58	−7.08	3.41	533	1999	1999
Chiron Corporation	NASDAQ	Hybrid	6	18	4,633.40	628.51	81.02	244.75	4,000	1981	1983
Genentech Inc.	NYSE	Therapeutics	8	17	23,169.56	906.53	215.76	337.71	3,883	1976	1980
MedImmune Inc.	NASDAQ	Therapeutics	2	6	6,837.62	193.77	−0.34	35.95	500	1988	1991
PE Corporation – PE Biosystems	NYSE	Technology platforms	N/A	N/A	9,374.17	758.14	109.16	66.52	3,915	1995	1999

Notes: LSE = London Stock Exchange. NYSE = New York Stock Exchange.

Currencies converted to € using year-end exchange rates.

*Financial figures for Axis-Shield for 9 months to end of December 1998 only.

**Celltech's one marketed drug (since its merger with Chiroscience) is Chirocaine. Celltech's Mylotarg received regulatory approval by the US Food and Drug Administration (FDA) in May 2000 and approval in Europe is likely later in 2000, but so far Mylotarg has not been marketed.

Sources: German, UK and US company websites; Dechema (2000); Hemington Scott (2000); Lehman Brothers (2000); E*Trade (2000); Merrill Lynch (1999, 2000); SG Cowen (2000a).

Table 2.3 **Products in the pipelines of European public biotechnology companies, 1999**

Country	Pre-clinical	Phase I	Phase II	Phase III
UK	29	28	36	11
Germany	2	–	–	–
France	4	5	4	–
Sweden	5	7	2	–
Denmark	5	1	6	–
Netherlands	–	1	1	–
Total	**45**	**42**	**49**	**11**

Source: Ernst & Young (2000), 5.

Still, within Europe, the UK leads by all criteria. The differences in employment, turnover, and research and development (R&D) expenditures point to important differences in maturity in Germany and the UK. According to Ernst & Young (2000, 12), 'two thirds of the value of European biotechnology is represented in the UK biotechnology sector'. More than two thirds of the therapeutics projects in the European public company pipelines are in UK companies. These companies are the only ones with products in Phase III. See Table 2.3.

Before the 1993 amendment to the Genetic Engineering Act, most commercial biotechnology in Germany was conducted in established major companies, above all in the pharmaceutical sector (Romanowski, 1999). Major pharmaceutical companies' contributions to the industry are not captured in our data that focuses on the dedicated biotechnology sector. According to the German Chemical Association, Dechema, two thirds of the biotechnology companies that currently exist in Germany have been founded in the years since 1993 (Dechema, 2000). See Figure 2.1.

Germany is catching up quickly with the UK in terms of the number of companies but remains far behind in terms of employment, R&D spend and number of public companies.

On a time line of the 'dedicated biotechnology industry' that starts in 1976 with the establishment of Genentech in the US, the first venture capital-backed biotechnology company, and continues to the pre-

Figure 2.1 **New biotechnology firm creation in Germany,
1980-1999**

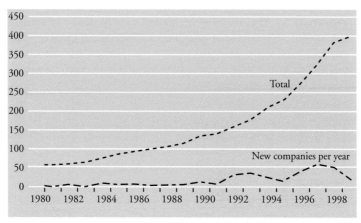

Source: Dechema (2000).

sent, the UK enters in 1980 with the founding of Celltech, and
Germany enters with the listing of Qiagen on NASDAQ in 1996. The
date of a country's entry into the industry impacts the size and maturity profile of its companies. As is discussed in Section 3, the size and
maturity profiles, in turn, help define the set of problems that companies (and policy makers) must deal with.

Germany's relative 'youth' is demonstrated by industry size and age
profiles. Schitag Ernst & Young (1998) estimated that as of late 1998
almost 60 percent of Germany's companies were less than two years
old. Figure 2.2 shows that in 1998 over 80 percent of German companies had fewer than 50 employees. A large percentage of UK companies are also still in the small and young categories, suggesting a
continuing start-up dynamic, but 42 percent have more than 50
employees and over 80 percent are more than five years old. See Figure
2.3.

Despite their earlier starts, however, few of the UK biotechnology
companies have managed to turn research projects into marketable
products or even to reach late stage clinical trials. According to the

Figure 2.2 **The size structure of German biotechnology and UK**
biopharmaceutical companies, 1998

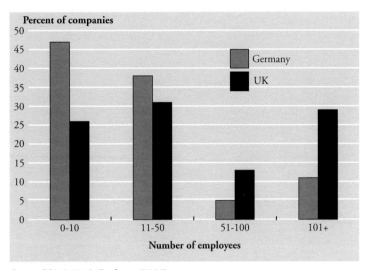

Sources: BIA (1999a); Dechema (2000).

product data on the Recombinant Capital website (Recombinant Capital, 2000), only ten of the 43 public UK companies have products in Phase III trials[6].

The biopharmaceutical industry has a range of sub-markets including therapeutics, diagnostic aids, and platform technologies designed to assist in the discovery of new therapeutics. Operating within these sub-markets, companies apply a range of business strategies. Some therapeutics producers aim to create fully integrated drug discovery companies, while others specialise in just the discovery phases. A third group develops a specific service or technology to 'sell' to other biotechnology and major pharmaceutical companies. Table 2.4

6 As many companies seek to license out compounds after Phase II clinical trials, this figure probably understates the value of the UK pipelines. To get a more accurate measure one would have to track the progress of products UK companies have licensed out. To measure the value contributed by technology providers to new drug development one would have to track their service deals.

Figure 2.3 **The age profile of German biotechnology and UK biopharmaceutical companies, 1998**

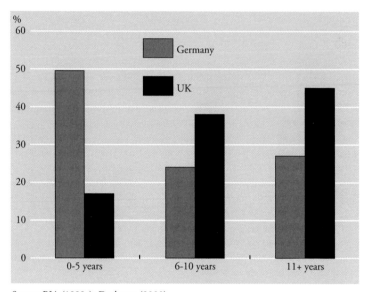

Sources: BIA (1999a); Dechema (2000).

describes some of the different business strategies.

Arthur Andersen's 1994 and 1997 surveys showed UK companies moving from fully-integrated business models towards platform technologies, licensing-out manufacturing, and virtual strategies[7]. See Figure 2.4. Reasons for shifting out of the fully integrated model include:

1. the companies' inability to raise the required large amounts of capital to bring products through clinical trials to market;
2. gaps in the companies' set of manager and staff competencies; and

---

7 In a virtual strategy, the company manages the move of compounds from Phase I of clinical trials through to market launch by way of contracts or joint ventures with third parties.

Table 2.4 **Biotechnology business models**   **25**

Strategy	Description
Fully integrated company	Company's activities span the entire range of operations from initial research through to marketing and distribution.
License-out manufacturing only	Company out-sources products for manufacture but manages all the other stages of the process the laboratory bench to the market.
License-out marketing only	Company licenses-out a developed and manufactured product to be marketed.
License-out manufacturing and marketing functions	Company researches and manages the development of products to a stage where they are ready for full-scale manufacturing and marketing by a third party. Development and pilot manufacturing skills can be accessed through partnerships but this requires an ability to manage third parties.
Virtual	Strategy requires fund-raising skills, expertise in licensing-in technology or products and taking those products through development to market by way of contracts or joint ventures with third parties.
Hybrid	Company applies its own technology towards the generation of therapeutic leads.
Technology for licensing ('toolbox')	Company focuses on R&D of a technology and licenses out the intellectual property to other companies.
Marketing only	Company provides sales and distribution networks for third parties' products. This needs some degree of R&D and manufacturing knowledge to provide technical support and service to end-users.

Source: Arthur Andersen (1997), 58-60.

3. the recognition that it is often cheaper and more efficient to let a 'specialist' do part of the work rather than try and learn and develop all stages in-house (Clement, 2000).

In their year 2000 report on Europe, Ernst & Young suggest that UK companies should continue to change strategies using alliances, mergers and acquisitions to move towards hybrid strategies and to add to their pipelines. In general Ernst & Young argue that, 'there is little room for the go-it-alone company in today's environment. Cross-licensing and alliances are the only way a company can efficiently meet all its technological needs' (ibid, 12).

Evidence about Germany's business strategies can be drawn from information about the companies' product segments and interviews. In terms of product segment, in a comparison of Germany and the UK, we find Germany concentrating on technologies and diagnostics. By contrast, a third of the UK products are in therapeutics. See Figure 2.5. Information from Dechema's annual surveys suggests a further

Figure 2.4 **UK biopharmaceutical strategy structure, 1994 and 1996**

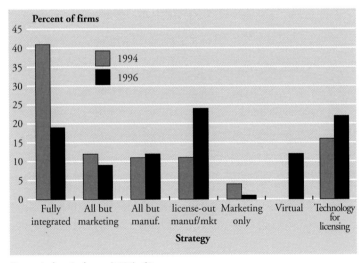

Source: Arthur Andersen (1997), 62.

Figure 2.5 **Product structures in Germany (1998) and the UK**   **27**
(1999)

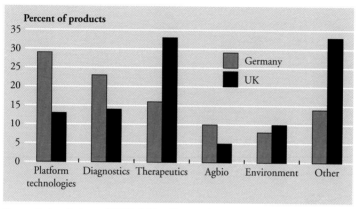

Sources: Arthur Andersen (2000); Schitag Ernst & Young (1998).

move in German company strategy between 1998 and 1999 towards service, technology, and diagnostic segments away from pharmaceuticals. See Figure 2.6.

According to the UK BioIndustry Association (BIA, 1999a), within the biopharmaceutical segment in the UK, about 20 percent of companies are developing new medicines and vaccines while the rest are developing diagnostic tests and undertaking R&D and consulting on a contract basis for other companies[8]. Information about German company strategy within the health care segment is not available.

The similarities between the German and UK biotechnology industries seem to stop at the number of companies. The UK industry has more mature companies, a broader range of company by size and product segment, and is more focused in therapeutics research. The young German industry has so far focused on platform technology and other service areas. The remaining sections seek to explain the sources of these differences. First we look at the basic set of compe-

8 Arthur Andersen 1998 figures would put the share of UK therapeutics companies at around 30 percent.

Figure 2.6 **Main business activities in German biotechnology companies**

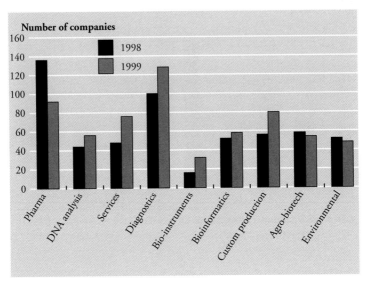

Source: Dechema (2000).

tencies that companies need to be able to operate in the global industry. Then we examine the extent to which and in what ways UK and German institutions support the building of these competencies.

3 THE DYNAMICS OF THE BIOTECHNOLOGY INDUSTRY

From a company's viewpoint, success involves turning a new start-up unit into a viable business. For a therapeutics or diagnostics company, this means gaining market approval and launching patented compounds, or doing profitable licensing deals with pharmaceutical firms at an earlier stage. For a technology producer it means finding enough customers to purchase or license their platform technologies to earn profits. For hybrid companies success entails some combination of these strategies. To measure progress in the sector at a national level, the number of companies earning profits, with products on the market and at a later stage of development, and with valuable deals with major pharmaceutical companies are better indicators of future development than the number of companies.

As the disappointing performance figures presented in Section 2 suggest, there are many obstacles to success, due to the complexity of the industry. Biotechnology companies must develop competencies to manage a number of relationships both within the firm and with external partners and around high-risk technologies whose developments are susceptible to failure. Furthermore, they must build these organisational structures and relationships within an uncertain strategic environment, in an industry where business models continue to change in response to scientific developments and changes in the needs of the major users, in particular the major pharmaceutical companies. Four features are specific to the biotechnology industry:

1. as is the case for the pharmaceutical industry in general, there is a high degree of risk involved in commercialising biotechnology research. In the biopharmaceutical sector it takes 10 to 15 years on average to bring a new compound to market and up to 80 percent of discoveries fail to make it. Hundreds of millions of Euros can easily be spent before scientists know whether a compound will succeed[9]. As this money tends to come from outside investors, these investors' money as well as scientists' and managers' jobs are at risk;

9 According to DiMasi et al. (1991), discovery and Phases I and II of clinical trials cost $263 million per approved new chemical entity on average.

2. the innovation process operates through a complex network of actors. The success of any company depends on its own in-house capabilities and resources, its ability to use the network's resources, and on supporting institutions being in place to ensure that the components of the network exist and can interact effectively. Furthermore, over the firm's growth lifecycle, the make-up of its network changes as its competency and resource requirements change;

3. the management of demand-side factors and, in particular, relationships between large pharmaceutical firms and dedicated biotechnology firms, are important. Large pharmaceutical firms comprise the primary market for most biotechnology firms, whether therapeutics or technology producers. As the major pharmaceutical companies undergo their own restructuring processes, their demands for new ideas and technologies from outside specialists change. Biotechnology companies must keep this in mind as they develop their own strategies.

4. the industry evolves over time. The state of the science, users' demands, and finance providers' expectations are all dramatically different in 2000 than they were in 1980. To succeed today, companies have to consider different business models with different types of networks from those required by their predecessors.

We discuss each of these four factors in turn.

3.1 High risks and costs

Biotechnology is a technology-driven industry where the likelihood of failure is high. Development times (from the date of first cloning, isolation or compound code assignment, to the date of first launch) for biotechnology products average 11 years (CMR International, 1999)[10,11]. On a global basis, only 18 percent of products entering

---

10 CMR International defines biotechnology products/projects as those therapeutic proteins expressed in bacteria, yeast, or animal cell systems, which can be manipulated using genetic engineering. This definition can also cover the components of gene therapy, whereby a defective gene is modified or replaced with a functional one. It is not limited to the projects currently underway in dedicated biotechnology companies.

Phase 1 of clinical trials are expected to make it to market launch, compared with 20 percent for non-biological products (CMR International, 1999). Specifically, between 1980 and 1998 development had ceased for 1,539 of the total 1,870 biotechnology projects which had been in development (excluding pre-clinical development) during that period. Again this represents an attrition rate of 82 percent (CMR International, 1999, 233). The surviving 331 projects are either still in development or have yielded a product approved for market. Figure 3.1 shows the distribution by phase of biological projects in development between 1995-1998.

As noted in Section 2, the marketable output of the global biotechnology industry has so far been disappointing considering the amount of money the hundreds of firms have invested to bring thousands of products to clinical trials. In 1998 alone, a total of 2,461 biotechnology companies in the US and Europe spent approximately €10.8 billion on R&D (Ernst & Young, 1999, 3). As of January 2000, only 90 drugs designed through biotechnology research techniques had been approved by the US Food and Drug Administration (FDA) (BIO, 1999a). This figure includes new indications for existing products.

Behind the strategies to invest in biotechnology facilities, license-in biotechnology products, do deals and acquire biotechnology companies, are the expectations on the part of major pharmaceutical companies that advances in biotechnology will help boost their product pipelines and number of patented products on the market (Ashton, forthcoming). Figure 3.2 shows the number of biotechnology products and other new molecular entities (NMEs) launched world wide between 1990 and 1999 by both biotechnology and major pharmaceutical companies. Biotechnology's share of all products

11 Ashton (forthcoming) finds that the average development times for biotechnology products launched between 1982 and 1997 were slightly shorter than those for non biotechnology products though the gap has narrowed over time. It was difficult to identify where the advantages lie but part of the difference may be linked to the fact that a high percent of the biotechnology products received FDA priority status and were fast tracked through the approval process.

Figure 3.1 **Biopharmaceutical products in development, world wide**

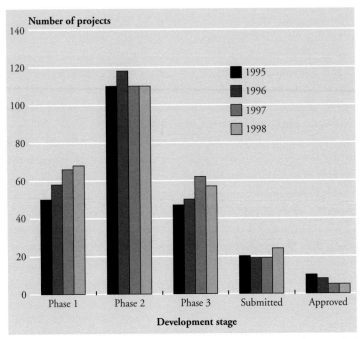

Notes: This figure includes projects in both biotechnology and major pharmaceutical companies.

Phase I clinical trials examine safety and pharmacokinetics in healthy volunteers.

Phase II clinical trials examine preliminary efficacy as well as safety and dosing.

Phase III clinical trials examine definitive efficacy and broader safety measures in a target patient population.

Submitted = registration documents submitted but not yet approved.

Approved = registration obtained but marketing not yet started.

Source: CMR International (1999), 236.

launched has fluctuated but has not, so far, made a sizeable contribution to total NME output. When approved products are categorised according to therapeutic category, however, biotechnology-based and non-biotechnology-based do seem to have different areas of focus. See Figure 3.3.

Figure 3.2 **Biotechnology-based products and other NMEs**
launched world wide, 1990-1999

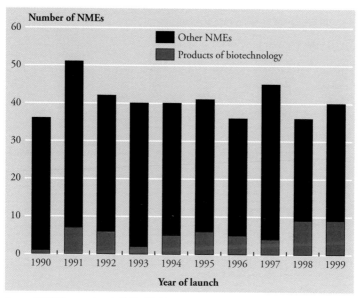

Source: CMR International, 2000, 10-13.

It is important to emphasise that the products included in CMR's sample are not limited to products launched by dedicated biotechnology companies. Of the 60 products in their sample launched onto the market between 1982 and 1998, dedicated biotechnology companies or research groups originated 44 percent of the approved products but have marketed only 18 percent of them. Traditional pharmaceutical companies originated 42 percent of the products and marketed 78 percent[12]. See Figure 3.4.

When products do make it to market few actually earn sufficient revenues to make a company self-financing. According to a study of a

12 Biotechnology companies are also not necessarily developing only biotechnology products. In 1998, for example, biotechnology companies filed six of the 30 FDA-approved chemical (i.e. non-biological) entities (Burrill & Co., 1999, 11).

34   Figure 3.3 **Biotechnology products and other NMEs launched 1992-1998, by therapeutic class**

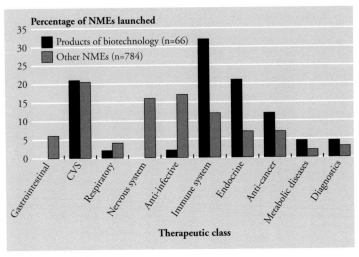

Source: Ashton (forthcoming).

sample of biotechnology products currently in development (in both major pharmaceutical and biotechnology companies), 'over three quarters of the biotechnology products for which information was provided are not expected to achieve peak sales of more than US$500 million' (Ashton, forthcoming, 26). For 1998, of the 15 products brought to market by biotechnology companies, 'four have the potential to become blockbusters (annual sales exceeding $500 million)' (Burrill & Co., 1999, 12). This means that, so far, only a handful of companies have managed to earn profits selling new biological entities: Amgen, Genentech, Biogen, Chiron, and Genzyme (Ernst & Young, 1998a).

According to data provided by Pharma Projects, 87 percent of the biotechnology research projects in development in 1998 were in just three therapeutic categories: anti-cancer; immunology; and, anti-infectives (CMR International, 1999). See Figure 3.5.

According to Figure 3.6, which compares the areas of research concentration in 42 global pharmaceutical companies (rather than specifically biotechnology companies) with those where products have been

Figure 3.4 **Types of companies originating and marketing**
biotechnology products world wide, 1982-1998

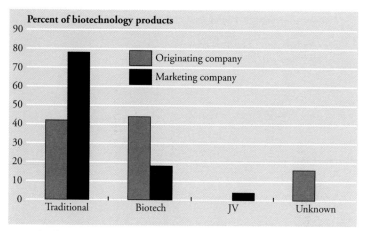

Note: This figure covers the 60 products launched onto at least one country of a 20-country market between 1982 and 1998. JV refers to a joint venture between a traditional and a biotechnology pharmaceutical company.

Source: CMR International, 1999.

launched, much of the research into anti-cancer and anti-infective treatments and the nervous systems has yet to bear fruit.

The high costs of drug R&D – estimated between $300 and $600 million per NME (Kettler, 1999) – and the high attrition rates mean many biotechnology start-ups will fail. The industry is well characterised by the term 'creative destruction'. Most biotechnology companies have narrow product portfolios, constrained by costs and resources to focus on one or two products. This puts them at high risk in the event of delays or unfavourable developments in clinical trials (Office of Technology Policy, 1997, 76). Due to the high failure rate of both projects and firms, there is high turnover of staff within companies and a constant process of start-ups, company reconfigurations, and shutdowns as scientists recombine research ideas and assets. The UK Department of Trade and Industry (DTI) estimates that only 35 percent of all UK start-up companies (not just biotechnology) will be

Figure 3.5 **Biopharmaceutical products in development by therapeutic class, 1998**

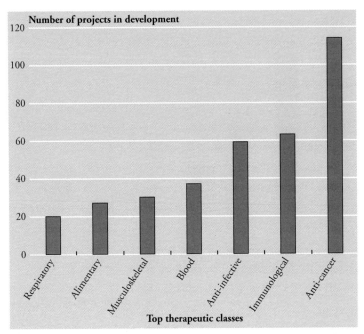

Note: 82 percent of the total 350 projects are included in these seven therapeutic classes. Some may be listed in more than one area.

Source: CMR International (1999), 242-243.

in existence at the end of their sixth year. However, evidence as to whether technology-based firms are more or less likely to fail than firms in more conventional sectors is inconclusive (Bank of England, 1996, 12).

3.2 Innovation over a network

A key feature of the biotechnology start-up is that its survival and growth depend on its successful interaction with a complex set of actors. Biotechnology is a network-based industry. Organisational theorists have suggested that in complicated, quickly changing technolo-

Figure 3.6 **Biotechnology products in research and on the market by therapeutic class, 1998**

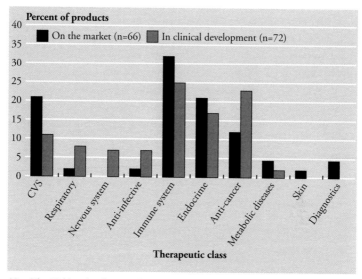

Note: The 72 biotechnology products in research are those in clinical development by a cohort of 42 global pharmaceutical companies (not biotechnology companies specifically) involved in Ashton's survey. The 66 biotechnology products on the market are from all pharmaceutical and biotechnology companies.

Source: Ashton, forthcoming.

gies such as biotechnology, small dedicated research units with considerable autonomy and high-powered performance incentives (stock options) may be more innovative than large, hierarchical organisations. However, specialisation entails that each firm must collaborate extensively with other parties to gain access to both complementary technologies and a variety of competencies necessary to develop and commercialise products.

Innovation in biotechnology is dependent on the flow of knowledge and people between university laboratories, start-up research firms, venture capitalists, public investors, and large pharmaceutical companies (Powell, 1999; Powell et al., 1996; Powell and Brantley, 1994). It is virtually impossible for biotechnology firms to go it alone.

Even companies that decide to try and bring their own compounds through clinical trials to market usually depend on research links with universities and other companies, finance and commercial advice from their investors, and so on. Key actors in the biotechnology network include: federal and state governments; universities; research institutions; technology transfer offices; venture capital providers; business angels; pharmaceutical firms; contract research organisations (CROs); service and supply providers; and, regulatory bodies.

Furthermore, the nature of any one company's network changes over the course of its development. Ernst & Young and Arthur

Figure 3.7 **The bioscience growth cycle**

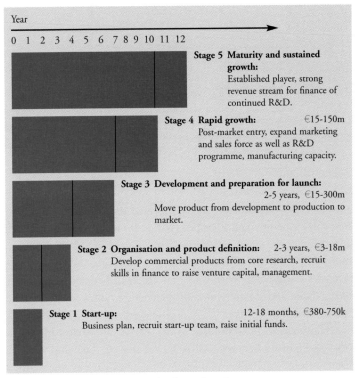

Note: Euro figures refer to estimates of each stage's total costs.
Source: Arthur Andersen (1997), 22.

Figure 3.8 **Providers of finance over the biotechnology firm lifecycle**

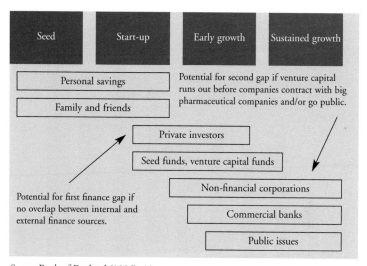

Source: Bank of England (1996), 13.

Andersen define the growth phases of the 'generic' biotechnology start-up in five phases (see Figure 3.7). The range of years and expense for each phase reflects the variety across product segments. Diagnostics and platform technology production, for example, would tend to be at the lower end of the cost and duration range and therapeutic products at the high end. Each of the phases can be identified by a set of activities (e.g. setting up a business plan, hiring managers, applying to business angels for first round funding in the start-up phase) and a distinct network. Over their growth cycle, companies have different driving concerns, deal with different types of financial providers, require different kinds of service providers and suppliers, seek to recruit managers and staff with different kinds of skills and so on. Figure 3.8, for example, shows how companies' financial requirements change over their lifecycle, as do the primary finance providers. The risk of failure for the investors also varies across the stages.

The key relationships developed in this report are those between biotechnology companies and technology suppliers (universities and

Figure 3.9a **Number of pharmaceutical alliances**

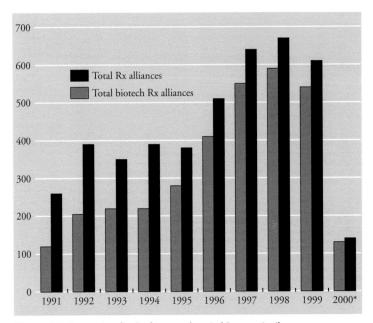

Notes: *2000 data are just for the four month period January-April.
Rx = Pharmaceutical companies.

Source: Copyright (2000) Windhover Information Inc. All rights reserved.

research laboratories), financial providers (venture capitalists, public investors), and important purchasers (major pharmaceutical firms). Technology transfer relationships and financing arrangements are discussed in Sections 4 and 5. Alliances with pharmaceutical firms are discussed in the next section.

3.3 Demand for biotechnology products – relationships with pharmaceutical companies

The importance of doing deals with major pharmaceutical companies has increased as biotechnology companies have moved away from the fully integrated strategy and diversified into the business of technolo-

Figure 3.9b **Total dollar volume of pharmaceutical alliances**

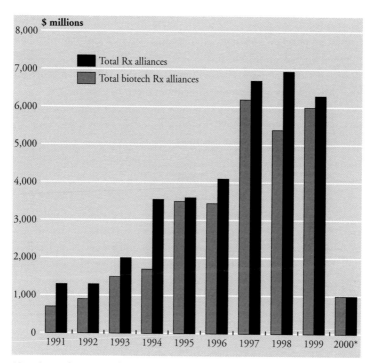

Notes: *2000 data are just for the four month period January-April.
Rx = Pharmaceutical companies

Source: Copyright (2000) Windhover Information Inc. All rights reserved.

gies as well as products. Figure 3.9a shows the development of alliances in the 1990s. The dollar value of those alliances has followed a similar pattern. See Figure 3.9b.

Pharmaceutical firms are primary users of the biotechnology companies' products, i.e. compounds that have been identified but not yet tested in humans, or new technologies used to discover new compounds. A number of pressures within the industry have driven major companies to look outside their own in-house research facilities. Due to 'increasing pressures from rising R&D costs, on the one hand, and constraints on revenues due to new cost containment health care policies on the other, large pharmaceutical companies have proved ready to look to external organisations to conduct specific stages of drug development' (Simpson, 1998, 16). In addition, the time between the first entry of a new medicine in a therapeutic area and the introduction of follow-on products in the same area is shortening (Towse and Leighton, 1999; Powell, 1996). This means that companies must get new drugs to the market more quickly in order to earn returns.

Pharmaceutical companies can use alliances to expand their range of product research. They 'develop in-house expertise at low costs in areas in which they lack capability by linking up with leading edge research and highly trained scientists in new biotechnology firms or public sector research' (Senker, 1996, 226)[13].

From the other side, collaborative research alliances provide biotechnology companies with access to their partners' complementary assets, including: 1. capabilities in clinical testing; 2. knowledge of how to comply with regulatory requirements; and, 3. well-developed marketing and distribution capabilities (ibid., 226). Partnerships allow biotechnology companies to specialise in discovery and early development and still earn revenues.

Alliances are a primary source of funding for ongoing R&D. These funds allow biotechnology companies to delay going public until they have better established portfolios of products in the pipeline, and so increase the chances that the initial public offering (IPO) will be successful. Having a record of good deals also improves a company's standing with venture capitalists and the investment community. In agreeing to establish an alliance, a large pharmaceutical company helps to validate the biotechnology company's claim that they have a marketable product (Platika, 1999; SG Cowen, 1998). Alliances cannot protect start-ups against all eventualities, however, as was evident during 1998 when even biotechnology companies with multiple strong

---

13 There is an extensive literature on strategic alliances in the biotechnology industry. Studies of alliances from the standpoint of major pharmaceutical companies include Sharp (1999), Senker (1996), and Arora and Gambardella (1990). Studies on the structure and learning benefits of alliances include Khanna et al. (1998), Lerner and Tsai (1999), Barley et al. (1994), and Stuart (1999).

partners saw their stock prices sink dramatically (Burrill & Co., 1999, 93).

Even with all the potential benefits arising from an alliance, biotechnology firms must manage important risks when forming deals with pharmaceutical firms. Small biotechnology firms run the risk of licensing extremely valuable intellectual property to pharmaceutical firms at rates far below market value at a later stage in development. The financial expenditures, or 'burn rate', of biotechnology firms can be tremendous, especially for therapeutics firms moving products into early stage clinical trials. This high rate of expenditure, coupled with long, oft-delayed development cycles with high failure rates, can play into the hands of large pharmaceutical firms looking to access new research ideas. Biotechnology firms must balance the need to build alliances for financial and reputation reasons with the ability to protect the market value of their projects by delaying the sale or licensing of intellectual property until its fullest possible market value can be obtained.

Shorter development times lessen this risk for most technology platform providers, though the relative ease of entry in this area of the market can create intense competition for common services that quickly bring down price-levels and profits. Furthermore, major pharmaceutical firms increasingly expect technology specialists to provide an integrated platform of services (computer support, initial testing) rather than just the technology (Ernst & Young, 1999).

Biotechnology companies are able to pursue successful licensing-out strategies in part because the demand for their research and products by pharmaceutical companies has increased. It remains to be seen, however, if these patterns of alliances and licensing are part of established pharmaceutical companies' long term strategies to deal with new technologies or if this is a temporary phase, taken to help companies fill pipeline and technology gaps while they build up their in-house capabilities[14].

The alliance data in Figure 3.10 suggest that pharmaceutical companies have tended to use alliances to get access to the discovery

---

14 The OHE in collaboration with CMR International is currently conducting a study on this question.

Figure 3.10 **Alliances between the top 20 pharmaceutical companies and biotechnology firms**

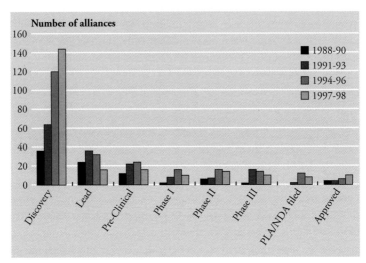

Source: Recombinant Capital (2000).

research and technologies in biotechnology companies and that the relative importance of discovery alliances has increased over time. This seems like good news for biotechnology companies.

But, while the focus has remained on early stage projects, a 1999 study by McKinsey & Company predicts the mix of alliances will change. 'Currently we are seeing a drop in the number of platform technology deals as major pharma seeks to assess and absorb the multiple technologies from recent investments' (Dewhurst et al., 1999, 66). This suggests that therapeutics and research companies will benefit in the future at the expense of technology producers. What is evident in any case is that biotechnology companies' ability to grow in the future through alliances will depend on how the pharmaceutical companies structure their R&D systems.

Finally, it is important to assess whether location-specific factors influence the formation of alliances. Through most of the 1980s and 1990s, the best research and the largest critical mass of biotechnology

companies and scientists were in the US and thus most alliances were   **45**
between US companies (Sharp, 1999). What is not clear is whether,
by missing out on the early wave of investments, European biotechnology companies are less attractive to major pharmaceutical companies now. Are there first-mover advantages for a country from the
standpoint of setting up alliances? Put another way, now that there are
German biotechnology companies, will German pharmaceutical companies, which invested substantial sums in research facilities in the US
in the 1980s, turn their attention to local companies? In selecting
companies for research alliances or deals of any kind, large companies
could be expected to look for the one with the best strategic fit and
that biotechnology company could be located anywhere. As a result,
emerging biotechnology firms in Europe that have developed high
quality projects should be able to form alliances. While numerous
alliances exist between large pharmaceutical companies and UK
biotechnology firms, the relative immaturity of the German industry
means that alliances there are only now beginning to be negotiated.

3.4 An industry changing over time

The different growth phases shown in Figure 3.7 are based on the fully
integrated strategy model where companies plan to conduct all stages,
from research through to marketing, in-house. Over time, developments in science and technology, changes in the way major pharmaceutical companies and other purchasers integrate these technologies,
and changes in the expectations of financial providers have all impacted upon the strategic-model decisions of companies:

1. *technology developments* – Over the past decade, a wide range of
   new platform technologies have been developed to help therapeutics companies discover new medicines. These include advances in
   gene sequencing technologies or genomics, combinatorial chem-
   istry, and bio-informatics.
2. *demand for biotechnology products and research* – Major pharmaceutical companies have come under increased pressure to reduce
   costs and get products to market more quickly. Trying to ratio-

nalise the drug discovery process, these companies have increasingly looked towards opportunities from new technologies and biology-based research methods. This, in turn, has led to significant amounts of resources being dedicated to collaborations with biotechnology companies (Henderson et al., 1998).

3. *market for high-risk finance* – Changes both inside and outside the industry have made investors more cautious about investing in the new biotechnology start-ups. The disappointingly slow pace of products launched, poor clinical trial results industry-wide, and the lack of UK success stories dampened investor enthusiasm for the UK sector in 1998 and 1999 (Burrill & Co., 1999). In general, investment funds and venture capital are shifting investments towards larger companies and, at least until a few months ago, were saving their high-risk investments for sectors where the expected return was quicker than in biotechnology, i.e. internet companies (Platika, 1999). As was mentioned earlier, investor attitudes towards biotechnology companies continue to fluctuate for reasons only partly to do with the industry itself (so called 'externalities').

These changes have had significant effects on the biotechnology sector. Most importantly, there has been a shift in company strategy away from the fully-integrated strategy, which many biotechnology companies and investors now consider too expensive and too risky (Arthur Andersen, 1997). Many companies are shifting towards front-end strategies – developing technology for licensing, or products, for others to manufacture and market. Others are using mergers and acquisitions to increase their size, fill out their pipelines, and broaden their technology scope (Ernst & Young, 2000).

Figure 3.4, on page 35, suggested that few companies have so far succeeded under the fully integrated company model as biotechnology companies have marketed only ten of the 60 biotechnology products launched between 1982 and 1998.

As we have already noted, new technological developments have created new market segments for biotechnology companies to exploit, particularly in platform technologies. Companies have developed a number of business models based around the provision of technology

Table 3.1 **Toolbox companies' performance**   **47**

Company	% change in stock price	
	1998	**May 1999 – May 2000**
Human Genome Sciences	–15%	+324%
Incyte	–16%	+346%
Affymetrix	–23%	+223%
Aurora Biosciences	–49%	+574%
Hyseq	–53%	+840%
Myriad Genetics	–63%	+565%
ArQule	–78%	+223%
Average change	*–42%*	*+442%*

Sources: Burrill & Company (1999), 111; E*Trade (2000).

services, such as contracting out patented technologies, drug discovery techniques and diagnostic tests. These markets have significantly lower short-term risks compared with those existing for product-oriented firms: R&D costs and capital requirements to get started are generally much smaller; lead times to bring products to market are shorter; and profits may be earned relatively quickly.

However, these toolbox technologies can quickly become commodities, subject to price competition. In the US, public investors' enthusiasm for platform technology companies continues to fluctuate widely. In 1998, the stock prices for the lead companies fell as adoption of their methods and development of drugs using their technology proved to be slower than predicted and profitability less robust than expected. 'Once the darlings of Wall Street, platform technology firms suffered through another bad year (1998) as they continued to report negative earnings and sceptics began to doubt the long term potential of their business model' (Burrill & Co., 1999, 106). Between May 1999 and May 2000, their values skyrocketed again, perhaps in response to positive progress reports from the Human Genome Project and to a reranking of the whole biotechnology sector. See Table 3.1.

To grow, platform technology firms must move relatively quickly into new technologies or towards discovering their own targets for development using their patented technology. As a result, a number of firms, particularly within the genomics technology segment, have developed hybrid strategies, focusing first on technology provision but then investing earnings into in-house therapeutics research (SG Cowen, 2000a).

3.5 Summary

To succeed in the biotechnology industry, companies must clear considerable scientific, managerial, organisational, and financial hurdles. As biotechnology and pharmaceutical companies have discovered, the time and money needed to develop new biotechnology-based medicines is equivalent to that needed for non-biotechnology products and the risks of failure are also just as high. It has also taken longer than many expected (hoped) to turn the information made available by new discovery technologies into marketable products. For biotechnology companies to operate at all, they must develop skills in network building and collaboration and their development in the short and medium term depends on their 'selling' their ideas and work-in-progress to venture capitalists and major pharmaceutical companies.

Biotechnology firms in the UK, Germany, and the US all operate under the industry conditions discussed in this section and yet, as outlined in Section 2, substantial differences exist in the structure and performance of these countries' industries. How can these country differences be reconciled? Time of entry might account for the different patterns of industry specialisation. Most German firms entered the industry later than many US and UK firms did, and therefore face different market and technological conditions than the earlier start-ups from the other countries. So, for example, it may not be surprising that more German firms are in the platform technology area. However, time cannot account for all the differences, and why were German firms so late to enter the market to begin with? Germany has one of the world's leading pharmaceutical sectors and a first class science base in the life sciences and yet its companies have yet to launch a biotechnology-based product. Moreover, why have UK companies failed to flourish despite following the strategic models of the industry leaders in the US – Amgen and Genentech?

These questions are addressed in the next three sections. We hypothesise that nation-specific institutional arrangements account for many of the differences in the performance and structure between Germany and the UK. We argue that the companies' product segments and strategy profiles as well as their performance records can be linked to differences in industry-specific and economy-wide institutions in the areas of technology transfer, finance and corporate governance, and the labour markets for scientists and managers. These institutions shape the innovative capabilities of companies in each country.

4 THE NATIONAL INSTITUTIONS APPROACH AND THE CASE OF TECHNOLOGY TRANSFER

4.1 Introduction to the national institutions approach

Analysts have long contrasted the organised nature of German or Rhineland capitalism with the more decentralised, market-centred Anglo-Saxon variety (see Albert, 1993; Dore et al., 1999; Hollingsworth, 1997; Soskice, 1997). In general, the UK has evolved into a liberal market-based system. Though considerable product regulations exist, markets for labour and finance are generally decentralised and deregulated. In Germany, powerful trade unions and industry associations still have significant collective organisational capacity, in particular with regards to the vocational training system, collective wage bargaining, and the governance of large firms through a stakeholder model of decision-making.

The broad differences in the market and in company organisation across the two countries have been linked to different national systems of innovation. German industry has been characterised as 'an innovation system which prefers to develop in-house capabilities and to build up competencies incrementally' (Momma and Sharp, 1999, 269). The UK innovation system, on the other hand, has been associated with the American model of fostering many radical innovations in new technologies, though the UK system is relatively less effective in their long-term commercialisation (see Vitols et al., 1997). Within this typology, the Anglo-Saxon model seems better suited to support the biotechnology sector which requires flexible labour markets for skilled researchers and managers, and investors willing and able to respond quickly to support risky ventures.

Our research supports the notion that Germany and the UK have widely contrasting patterns of market regulation and company organisation. However, seemingly contrary to the predictions of the national systems perspective, Germany has exhibited extensive dynamism in the biotechnology industry of late, at least in terms of creating new companies and attracting new investments while the UK performance has been sluggish. Thus, a detailed analysis of the relationship between

the countries' specific institutions, and the kind of institutional sup-   **51**
port companies need to succeed, is called for. While the management
of firms has wide discretion in crafting particular strategies, we suggest
that institutions strongly influence the resources or tool kits that firms
have at their disposal. We have found that while formal laws have
some influence, the most important role of institutions is in the broad
structuring of the financial and labour markets that small technology
firms must draw upon in order to create important competencies.

In this and the following two sections, we discuss three major areas
of competency construction: technology transfer; finance; and managerial and scientific labour markets. In each case we first discuss the
problems that institutions must try to address, using examples of institutional arrangements from the US case, the industry leader, and then
examine the particular institutional factors and obstacles in the UK
and Germany.

4.2 Technology transfer – the issue

In high-technology industries, the successful commercialisation of
research depends in part on a range of technology policies that facilitate the creation of entrepreneurial start-up firms, often spin-offs from
universities (Nelson and Rosenberg, 1994). With regard to the supply
of technology for biotechnology firms, the strength of the country's
life-sciences research base is clearly a critical factor. The presence of a
strong national science base, often supported by public funds, is therefore important both as a source of technology and as a source of training for skilled manpower (Momma and Sharp, 1999, 269).

The US lead in the biomedical basic science fields is clear. The
extensive federal funds distributed through the National Institutes of
Health (NIH) and other government programmes are a major factor
explaining the dominant position of the US biotechnology industry.
In 1999, for example, the NIH supported $697.5 million worth of
awards in bioengineering up from $501.1 million in 1998 (NIH,
2000). Research shows that Germany and the UK are in competition
for second place world-wide and for the lead spot in Europe, both in
terms of aggregate funding for biomedical research and in terms of

publications in biomedical fields (Momma and Sharp, 1999). According to a Science Watch study in 1992, Germany had nine universities and research institutions ranked in the top performance class while the UK had eight. UK citations per institution were higher though at 28.4, above Germany's 24 and the US's 21.9 (ibid., 271).

To exploit this science base commercially, however, institutions must also be in place to facilitate the transfer of technology from the public to the private sector. In the biotechnology sector, extensive finance and time investments are needed before the commercial relevance and market potential of basic life sciences research can be assessed. University laboratories are rarely in a position to develop promising research results into commercial products, and must rely on spin-off projects or licensing arrangements with established firms. For all biotechnology products launched between 1982 and 1998, academic organisations discovered less than 5 percent and marketed none of them (Ashton, forthcoming). At the other end of the network, major pharmaceutical companies commonly require evidence of potential marketability from the biotechnology research before they are willing to invest in it.

Collaborations between university laboratories and biotechnology firms emerge to commercialise new discoveries and technologies. Technology transfer practices in biotechnology must extend beyond simple licensing protocols to include an array of resources and incentives to encourage scientists to seek patents to cover the intellectual property generated within basic research laboratories. In the US, technology transfer programmes have often been combined with the development of local incubator laboratories and technology parks surrounding basic research campuses. University scientists also have at their disposal an array of financial and consulting resources they can use to patent research, to develop business plans for spin-off firms, and to arrange collaborations with existing biotechnology firms[15].

Intellectual property laws, national rules governing the transfer of public research to the private sector, and the financing of technology transfer offices within public universities and laboratories all influence

15 See the BIA's 'Mission to the USA' (1999b) for a description of the Maryland and North Carolina clusters.

how university administrators and scientists develop technology trans-   **53**
fer offices and practices. These rules and programmes differ between
countries, with important implications for how technology is supplied
to biotechnology firms.

In the US, university technology transfer has been regulated by the
Bayh-Dole Act since 1980. This law cedes ownership of all federally
funded research grants from the NIH and other funding sources to the
universities. This gives universities an incentive to set up technology
transfer offices to organise licensing or, in some cases, sponsor start-up
firms spun out of their university laboratories. Though revenue-shar-
ing arrangements differ across universities, it is common practice for
technology transfer offices to split income between the inventor scientist, his or her department, and the university. In order to foster the
participation of university scientists in technology transfer activities,
the Bayh-Dole Act established 20 percent as the minimum share in
royalties payable to inventing scientists engaged in federally-funded
research (Zucker and Darby, 1999).

The organisation of technology transfer systems is an important
policy issue in both Germany and the UK. In the two sections that follow we identify the important institutional differences across the two
countries and discuss recent attempts to embed university-firm technology transfer links within a broader regional cluster policy framework. These attempts include support for incubator laboratories and
technology parks to house agglomerations of local firms and specialised service providers such as patent lawyers.

4.3 Technology transfer in Germany

In the 1980s and early 1990s, the small firm spin-off dynamic that had
become commonplace within the US biotechnology sector did not
take place in Germany. Universities and research institutes conducted
biomedical science research with minimal commercial spin-offs activity. German professors were generally not seen as motivated to
become entrepreneurs. Momma and Sharp (1999) attribute German
university professors' antipathy 'to entrepreneurial activity, to their status as civil servants with considerable freedom and security' (270).

This attitude on the part of professors must at least partly be attributed to the lack of technology transfer resources and incentives provided to them by universities. Because universities in Germany do not own the intellectual property resulting from most research, they have had little incentive to establish technology transfer offices[16].

Under German law, professors own most intellectual property derived from publicly funded research. However, professors generally did not have the resources to obtain patents for this research and, until very recently, tended only to develop long-term relationships with established pharmaceutical companies rather than try to patent and commercialise it themselves. Intellectual property derived from such collaboration was usually transferred from university laboratories to large firms at no cost in return for consulting fees paid to professors. The relationship between universities and the private sector is strong, therefore, but the primary technology link has been with large firms[17].

In the mid 1990s, the German federal government introduced policies designed to create technology transfer mechanisms to better exploit university research, specifically by way of entrepreneurial spin-offs. Biotechnology was explicitly targeted (see Cooke, 1999).

The federally funded BioRegio competition, initiated in 1995, encouraged German regions to establish biotechnology promotion offices, as this was a prerequisite for consideration in the competition. The prize for the three winners of the competition was DM50 million in federal grants over a five-year period for the biotechnology office to use to support the development of local biotechnology industries.

16 One exception is the Max Planck Society, which due to its separate legal status has been able to control intellectual property within its laboratories and, through its technology transfer office, Garching Innovation, organizes licensing schemes based on the US model. Between 1979 and the end of 1998, Garching Innovation was the patent agent for 1,469 inventions and concluded 827 licensing agreements with firms abroad. In the last five years Garching Innovation has also run a separate programme to help organize spin-off firms from Max Planck laboratories. More than 20 companies have been established, the majority of them in the biomedical field (Max Planck Society, March 1999).

17 This paragraph relies strongly on the extensive review of German technology transfer practices in Abramson et al., 1997; see also Momma and Sharp, 1999 and Schmoch, 1999.

Specifically, the government funds were to be used to finance the **55** development of local technology transfer offices and fund pre-commercial R&D projects in local start-up firms. The competitors had to demonstrate that state and local grants as well as contributions from prominent local businesses and publicly managed venture capital funds would also be available to match federal funds.

The competition winners were Munich, the Neckar Rhine region (centred in and around Heidelberg), and Nordland Westphalen (primarily the Cologne area). The competition helped to jump-start the other regions as well. In addition to the money they all received to help set up the promotion offices in the first place, all of the regions whether competition winners or not, by virtue of their having participated in the competition, automatically qualified for state and local level grants. Berlin has also been able to tap into funds designated for post-German-unification restructuring and is the best example of a thriving, non-winning region. The map in Figure 4.1 shows the locations of all the biopharmaceutical companies (about one-third of the total number of biotechnology companies) in Germany as of January 2000. Included are the major pharmaceutical companies such as Bayer AG (Wuppertal) and Schering AG (Berlin). Figure 2.1 (page 22) showed that the number of new specialised biotechnology companies in Germany increased significantly in 1996, 1997, and 1998.

The numbers of small and medium sized enterprises (SMEs) in all biotechnology industry segments as of July 1998 for the regions that originally applied for the BioRegio funds are listed in Table 4.1. The winning regions are in bold.

The government-funded technology programmes have developed many of the functions typically conducted in university technology transfer offices in the US. In return for services and support, fledgling start-ups cede small equity stakes to either the local BioRegio office itself, or in some cases to para-public venture capital organisations operating in conjunction with the local programmes.

The BioRegio offices then draw upon a number of publicly funded programmes to help scientists and local entrepreneurs organise virtually every phase of start-up formation within the biotechnology sector. This includes:

Figure 4.1 **Location of biotechnology companies in Germany**

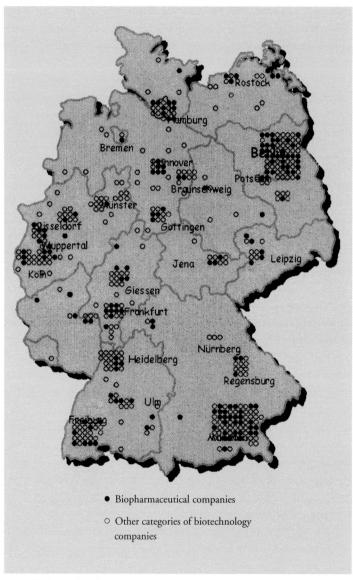

• Biopharmaceutical companies

○ Other categories of biotechnology
  companies

Source: Dechema (2000).

Table 4.1 **Biotechnology SMEs in Germany**   **57**

Region	Number of SMEs 1998	Start-ups since 1996
Berlin-Brandenburg	40	30
Braunschweig, Goettingen, Hanover	>30	25
Bremen	2	1
Freiburg	30	11
Greifswald-Rostock	17	7
Halle-Leipzig	13	7
Jena	>20	14
Mittelhessen	7	2
Munich	**36**	**16**
Nord (Hamburg, Kiel)	30	12
NW Niedersachsen	5	5
Regensburg	13	11
Rhineland (Cologne, Dusseldorf)	**50**	**11 (plus 8 company expansions)**
Rhine-Main Hessen	24	8
Rhine-Main Mainz	24	8
Rhine-Neckar-Triangle (Heidelberg)	**20**	**9**
Stuttgart	11	7
Ulm	8	4

Sources: British Embassy in Germany (2000); DTI/ British Embassy in Germany (1998).

1. hiring consultants to help university professors and their students commercialise their research and design viable business plans;
2. subsidies to help reduce the costs of patenting intellectual property; and,
3. management consulting and partnering advice to help companies create contacts with other actors in the local biomedical areas. Most of the BioRegio programmes have used public funds to create incubator laboratories to house fledgling start-ups in and around universities or public research laboratories. Several areas have also created technology parks to where firms can locate once they enter the expansion phases (Interviews, 1999).

Many commentators and industry reports have attributed the new institutional support for entrepreneurial biotechnology firms in Germany to the success of the BioRegio programmes (Momma and Sharp, 1999; Silvia, 1999; Schitag Ernst & Young, 1998; Ernst & Young, 1999). Given the long history of successful association activities within Germany, the government's success in fostering strong technology transfer linkages should not seem surprising. In the past, Germany has excelled in creating para-public association bodies to bridge the public and private sectors, for example, the vocational training system and organisation of collective R&D diffusion projects for small SMEs through the Frauenhofer and related organisations (Katzenstein, 1987, 1989). However, as our discussion of financial institutions in Section 5 makes clear, a balance between public support and market incentives is needed in order for the new commercially oriented start-ups to excel in the market place.

4.4 Technology transfer in the UK

While the German government's involvement in the commercialisation of biotechnology only really started in 1995, the UK government became involved in the active promotion of university-based spin-offs in the early 1980s. Celltech, the UK's first biotechnology firm, was established in 1980 as part of an initiative of the public National Enterprise Board (now the British Technology Group). This direct government involvement was exceptional. In general, UK technology transfer policies have been oriented towards the US model where national policy is designed to create a variety of legal and regulatory incentives to encourage universities, venture capitalists, and service oriented firms to organise biotechnology start-ups themselves. Direct public financial support of technology transfer institutions has been limited.

In 1985 the UK government reformed national laws regarding the exploitation of publicly funded research. Strongly influenced by the success of the US Bayh-Dole Act, the ownership of university intellectual property arising from publicly-funded academic research was transferred from the then government-owned British Technology

Group[18] to universities (Arthur Andersen, 1998). Universities were **59**
charged with the development of technology transfer offices that were
obliged to exploit and protect this intellectual property. This led to
the development of a number of technology transfer models within
UK universities, all of which operate on the basic principle of sharing
licensing revenues between individual scientists, their university
departments, and the university[19].

Though similar in design to the US, the results of the UK government technology transfer policies have lagged behind because of differences in the financial arrangements at the universities. UK
universities generally lack the large private endowments that have been
generated by alumni and corporate sponsors within large American
research universities. These endowments have proved crucial to
staffing large technology transfer offices in US research universities as
well as providing seed money to university-based venture capital funds
(Abramson et al., 1997, 82). In the long-term, UK technology transfer offices hope to generate substantial revenues from the licensing of
intellectual property, but in the short-term they must rely on funds
provided by the university. With insufficient funds, these offices
struggle to recruit enough high quality staff to appraise project proposals, and to provide the seed capital needed for investments in the
development of many projects (Arthur Andersen, 1998). The inability to pay a reasonable salary in the key area of technology transfer is a
major obstacle to it being successful in the UK. Technology transfer
salaries are less than half their US counterparts and are below even UK
academic counterparts (Clement, 2000).

Recent governmental initiatives could lead to more cohesion within UK technology transfer offices. The most important of these programmes is the University Challenge Fund (UCF), introduced in 1998.
This programme invites university technology transfer offices to submit
bids for between £1 and £5 million of seed capital funding for start-up
firm projects organised through the university. The programme aims

18 The British Technology Group was privatized via an employee and manager buy-out
in 1992 (BTG website, www.btgplc.com, January 23, 2000).
19 For an excellent discussion of this see Arthur Andersen's 1998 report *Technology
Transfer in the UK Life Sciences*.

to create incentives for greater co-operation between university technology transfer offices, local venture capitalists, and existing firms within particular regions. It mandates that two-thirds of the members of the UCF governing boards within each university be non-academics. It also requires each university to obtain matching grants of 25 percent of the total requested from governmental funds, ideally from venture capitalists, industry angels, and firms. While the UCF is open to all technological areas, the Wellcome Trust, a substantial private sponsor of biomedical research in the UK, has promised to match the initial governmental funding of £20 million, thereby ensuring that substantial UCF resources will flow to biotechnology projects.

In 1998 and 1999, the organisation of cluster support infrastructures became an important topic of discussion within UK biotechnology policy circles. The results of a fact-finding mission to examine the UK and US biotechnology clusters, led by Lord Sainsbury of Turville, were published in August 1999 (Sainsbury et al., 1999). The group's key recommendations to support the UK clusters included:

1. Harmonisation of intellectual property rules across different research organisations;
2. Competitions, held by universities in conjunction with venture capitalists and other sponsors, to stimulate science and management students to become entrepreneurs;
3. Improvements in the stock option packages companies can offer their employees; and
4. Financial support to regional biotechnology associations to help link together companies in their respective areas.

The US served as the basis for comparison in the Sainsbury-led study but references to the German BioRegio programmes were also made. In terms of what the UK can learn from the German experience, in the specific context of technology transfer, it is important to emphasise the different incentives facing university administrators and scientists in the two countries. The BioRegio programmes were designed largely to compensate for the lack of incentives facing German university administrators to commercialise research (i.e. they do not own publicly-funded intellectual property), while simultane-

Figure 4.2 **Biotechnology 'clusters' in the UK**

Note: Solid dots represent locations of biotechnology companies quoted on the London Stock Exchange, the Alternative Investment Market or Ofex. Others represent public centres of research and pharmaceutical R&D and manufacturing sites.

Sources: Based on Ernst & Young (1999) as modified by the authors to indicate the quoted companies.

ously introducing resources for the systematic development of small entrepreneurial technology firms. The leading technology clusters in the UK (Cambridge and Oxford) already have services similar to those recently set up by government-funded programmes in Germany. The map in Figure 4.2 shows the local concentration of the UK specialist biotechnology companies around Oxford, Cambridge and London and in the Glasgow-Edinburgh region of Scotland. Rather than set up new services, attention might be better placed on funding the existing facilities.

UK government programmes such as the UCF have been less pervasive in part perhaps because universities already have some incentive to organise major aspects of technology transfer infrastructures themselves[20]. Private actors in the UK have developed many of the services needed for entrepreneurial technology firms. This includes business plan consulting, the maintenance of technology parks, and, more recently, the development of business incubators closely tied to university laboratories.

Overall, promoters of current UK policy expect that the pervasiveness of private actors in the technology transfer and firm start-up systems in the UK, particularly venture capitalists, will lead to more successful (marketable) appraisals of proposals. The UCF and other recent UK technology push programmes provide financial incentives for universities to systematically include venture capitalists and established entrepreneurs or business angels in business plan competitions and in the early-phase development of firms linked to university research[21]. It is not immediately clear whether the more interventionist technology transfer policies that have been used in Germany are needed, or would be effective, in the UK.

20 It might also be the case that the amount of money available through these programmes is not sufficient to make a significant difference.
21 Experience suggests that there is a high correlation between a company successfully getting through to IPO and active hands on venture capitalists who are involved from the start-up stage. The relative abundance of money available in the UK for start-ups may hide weaknesses in the business model that are not exposed until venture capitalists apply tough objective reviews at a later stage (Clement, personal communication, May 2000).

5 FINANCE

5.1 Financing biotechnology – the issue

Over the growth lifecycle, companies seek out finance from different types of investors. A typical firm obtains funds from business angels and personal resources in the start-up phase, venture capitalists and non-financial corporations (e.g. large pharmaceutical companies) in the early growth and development stage, and public capital markets in the later growth and maturity stages. The key challenge is for the companies to be able to maintain R&D activities over the relatively long periods before their products reach the market (Florida and Kenney, 1986). Arthur Andersen (1997) estimates that over the start-up and early development phases alone a company needs somewhere between €3-20 million depending on their product focus.

The ability of a particular country to foster high-risk biotechnology firms is strongly correlated with the existence of financial institutions and markets geared towards the creation of equity-leveraged growth strategies. At issue is whether companies with all or most of the right ingredients – patented technology, the right mix of technological and wider business expertise in the management team, together with a convincing business plan and marketing strategy – are able to obtain finance on affordable terms.

The creation of financial market institutions to support equity-based growth strategies must be supplemented by general market confidence in the ability of financial and industry analysts to assess and govern the projects that go public. Individual or institutional investors will often take a portfolio approach but they must have confidence that the expected return across the portfolio is commensurate with the investments' assessed risks. Equity investors must have easy exit options before they will agree to invest in biotechnology companies. Knowing that the investors can (and will) use this option if they become nervous, puts continual pressure on managers in biotechnology firms that have gone public to demonstrate at key milestones that their projects have real prospects for future growth and earnings that justify the large capital investments.

Investors need success stories to keep them interested in the biotechnology sector. Though the majority of companies in the US are making losses, successful product developments by a few companies such as Amgen and Genentech have pushed the biotechnology share index along. High profile, high value purchases by large pharmaceutical companies of biotechnology companies such as Pharmacia & Upjohn's purchase of Sugen and Warner Lambert's purchase of Agouron have also been important. See Figure 5.1.

In Europe, where the industry is relatively young and there are no products on the market, investors must react to company news and the expectation of returns – i.e. clinical trial results, deals, mergers and acquisitions. After almost 12 months of stagnant or declining share prices, enthusiasm for the industry as a whole resumed in late 1999, fuelled in part by products launched in the US, new scientific breakthroughs in the human genome project, and hopes for product launches in the UK. It may have also reflected spillover effects from high gains in other technology sectors. In general, however, sector analysts such as SG Cowen (2000b) and Warburg Dillon Read (2000a) are still cautious about assessing the real value of the UK companies and especially the new public companies elsewhere in Germany. Ultimately, how high the company share price is and how fast it is changing is only important to the extent that it impacts attitudes of venture capitalists and public investors and their decisions to invest money in the sector.

In Germany and the UK there are nation-specific obstacles to obtaining finance for biotechnology firms. As in the case of technology transfer, the UK has market-based finance provision systems in place, but recurring performance disappointments suggest that something is not working correctly. Part of the problem may be the lack of confidence in the ability of venture capitalists and the broader financial community to adequately screen investments. Furthermore, the tax breaks available to motivate entrepreneurs and investors to take risks may still be inadequate. In the case of Germany, until recently there was almost no high-risk equity capital available for biotechnology. The structure of German finance and company laws shaped a financial system where banks and retained earnings have traditionally been the primary sources of finance, thereby ruling out industries such as biotechnology, where companies need high-risk equity finance. This is now changing.

Figure 5.1 **American Stock Exchange Biotechnology Index**   **65**
(BTK), October 1989-July 1998

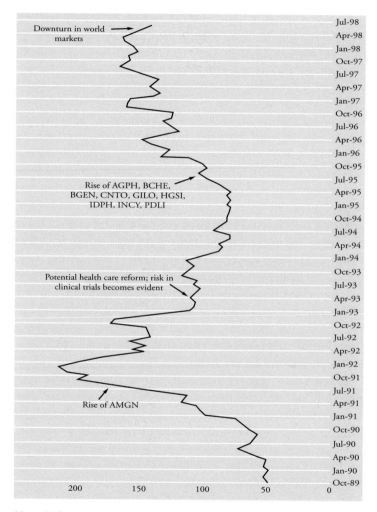

Notes: AMGN=Amgen Inc.; AGPH=Agouron Pharmaceuticals Inc.; BCHE=BioChem Pharma Inc.; BGEN=Biogen Inc.; CNTO=Centocor Inc.; GILD=Gilead Sciences Inc.; HGSI=Human Genome Sciences Inc.; IDPH=Idec Pharmaceuticals Corporation; INCY=Incyte Pharmaceuticals Inc.; PDLI=Protein Design Labs Inc.

Source: SG Cowen (1998, 40).

5.2 Financial markets in Germany

Until the late 1990s, substantial legal hurdles combined with the credit-based orientation of financial markets posed high obstacles to the systematic financing of high-risk technology firms through equity-leveraged financial schemes.

A primary obstacle was the absence of an active market for corporate control. A number of factors help to explain why such a market had not developed in Germany. Germany's consensus-oriented system of corporate governance, which gives statutory voting rights on company boards to groups of employees and other stakeholders, limits the power of shareholders (although this is more relevant for large companies than small ones). Specifically, because it grants substantial rights over the governance of public firms to employees, trade unions, and other major stakeholders, German company law limits the ability of shareowners to design the incentives and broad strategies given to top managers. The market for corporate control has also been limited by shareholdings being concentrated in the hands of large German commercial banks and other large companies through stable cross-shareholding and the extensive use of proxy-voting arrangements. This lack of flexibility has limited the development of equity models of financing in Germany, motivating companies to primarily use debt-based financing for investments (see Vitols et al., 1997; Carlin and Soskice, 1997; Edwards and Fischer, 1994).

These factors together motivated German firms to traditionally finance R&D and other speculative investments with retained earnings. Share offerings have not served as a primary source of funding for German firms, large or small. Compared to the US or the UK, Germany is still primarily a bank-centred financial system. At the end of 1997, German market capitalisation was 39 percent of Gross Domestic Product (GDP) compared to 155 percent in the UK and 129 percent in the US (Deutsche Bundesbank, 1998). Kettler sums up differences in ownership structures as follows: 'The majority of shares in Germany and Japan are held by committed shareholders, while shares in the US and UK are controlled by investors with shorter time horizons. While non-financial institutions are important in both

Germany and the US, corporate investors are key in Germany while   **67**
households dominate in the US. Banks are the most important type of
financial investor in Germany versus pension funds in the US and UK'
(Kettler, 1997, 229)[22].

The lack of developed capital markets in Germany, at least until
quite recently, implied a lack of experienced public investors willing to
invest in risky IPOs for technology firms. This, in turn, discouraged
venture capitalists from participating. While venture capitalists may
take stakes in firms, they have limited scope to organise preferential
shareholder rights, given that German corporate laws favour the rights
of employees, particularly during bankruptcy proceedings (Vitols et
al., 1997). Moreover, if share offerings cannot easily be supported on
domestic equity markets, then the exit option for venture capitalists is
limited to merger and acquisition activities or, perhaps, in cases of
extremely successful firms, listing on foreign stock markets.

The funds from IPOs should be an important source of finance.
Without these, companies must return to the original investors to
obtain new funds, something that venture capitalists are unlikely to
agree to given their short-time horizons. Moreover, without the possibility of quick returns created by IPOs, venture capitalists have more
difficulty diversifying risks through a portfolio strategy.

Entrepreneurial firms, in general, and biotechnology start-ups in
particular, have benefited from a set of reforms to the German financial markets implemented in the late 1990s. These reforms were
designed to relieve international competitive pressures on large
German companies. Under the new laws, companies were able to
incentivize employees more effectively and thereby increase the performance of the firm. While large German firms continue to be gov-
erned predominantly through a stakeholder model of company law,
the companies have worked to broaden their shareholder base through
sales of shares on international markets. They have also introduced
stock-option schemes and other mechanisms to motivate interest in
public capital markets.

22 Caution must be exercised when making international comparisons of
shareholdings as investor categories can mean different things or play different roles in
different countries (Kettler, 1997, 229).

Table 5.1 **Biotechnology IPOs on the Neuer Markt in 1999**

Company	Month	Nationality
MorphoSys AG	March	German
Rhein Biotech AG	April	German
MWG Biotech	May	German
Sanchochemica Pharmazeutica	May	Austrian
Evotec BioSystems AG	November	German

Source: Ernst & Young (2000), 16.

In late 1997 a NASDAQ-modelled stock exchange for technology companies, the Neuer Markt, was created by the privately owned Deutsche Boerse to supplement the blue-chip DAX-based segment of the Frankfurt Stock Exchange. This was followed, in March 1998, by a government-sponsored financial reform that allows publicly traded firms to buy and sell their own shares. This market has successfully supported several dozen equity listings of German firms in other technology sectors, as well as a secondary listing for the German-Dutch biotechnology company Qiagen, a platform technology specialist. Venture capitalists and investment bankers interviewed during our research considered the Neuer Markt to be Europe's most liquid small technology-centred stock exchange. In 1999 alone, four German and one Austrian biotechnology company launched successful IPOs on the Neuer Markt. See Table 5.1.

Capital gains tax reforms have also helped encourage business angels and retail investors to invest in technology firms. Investors who hold onto company shares pre- and post-IPO on the Neuer Markt for at least 12 months pay no capital gains (Clement, 2000).

Since 1996 the German federal government has worked to create incentives to stimulate the development of a venture capital market for high-risk technology firms. One move has been the provision of public venture capital in the form of sleeping or silent equity partnerships from federal sources to match private sources. Another is to offer generous capital gains tax breaks to investors.

Figure 5.2 **German 'public venture capital' of the tbg by sector,**   **69**
1996-1999

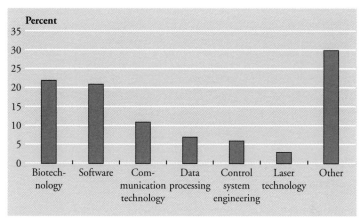

Source: tbg, 1999.

The public agency that oversees the public venture fund programme, the Technologie-Beteiligungs-Gesellschaft Gmbh (tbg),
invested more than €713 million in new technology start-up firms
between 1996 and 1999. By sector, biotechnology firms were recipi-
ents of the largest amount, receiving €153 million (22 percent) of tbg's
venture capital investment between 1996 and 1999 (tbg, 2000). See
Figure 5.2.

To increase their leverage and reduce the risk of opportunism, federal funds have generally been offered only when firms can obtain
matching funds from lead private investors. Lead investors are commonly private venture capital firms, but also include banks. Firms with
matching funds are awarded favourable lending terms. At any time
during the initial seven years following the deal, the firm can buy back
the tbg shares. This means that successful firms can repurchase shares
at low initial valuations and reissue them in more profitable private
placements or in preparation for going public. At the same time the
federal government writes off the losses incurred by failures.

Companies can supplement federal funds with an array of local

Table 5.2 **Seed-finance in the Munich BioRegio**

	€ million
Lead investment by BioM AG	0.15
Private investors	0.15
Silent partnership (tbg)	0.30
Silent partnership (Bayern Kapital)	0.30
Total	**0.90**

Source: DTI/British Embassy in Germany (1998).

Table 5.3 **Genome Pharmaceuticals Corporation seed- and start-up financing**

	€ million
Private venture capital financing (1997)	3.3
State and governmental silent partnerships and grants (1998)	
– Bavarian state funding (Bayern Kapital)	2.6
– Federal funding (tbg)	2.6
– BioRegio research grant	2.8
Total	**11.3**

Source: Genome Pharmaceuticals Corporation (2000).

grants, loans, and subsidies co-ordinated through their regional technology transfer offices. These grants are usually given in tandem with federal equity partnerships, creating in effect a triple leveraging of private investments for many biotechnology start-ups. A recent study of German public venture capital found that 'when combined with matching seed and other funding on soft terms from within each state, the leverage of Federal schemes can be as high as 1:5, not counting additional grants for research projects' (Barnett et al., 1998, 29). To give some indication of the amount of leverage available, Table 5.2 shows the kind of seed capital a single company winning approval from the Munich BioRegio co-ordinator, BioM AG, can receive. The second chart, Table 5.3, shows the financial structure during the seed

financing round of one of Munich's leading biotechnology firms, **71**
Genome Pharmaceuticals Corporation (GPC).

The combination of substantial public subsidies with generally sophisticated technology transfer offices focused around German biomedical research centres has led to an explosion of start-up firms over recent years. The German public venture capital has steered much of German venture capital activity into seed-capital projects. It is still too early however, to assess whether these start-ups will survive in the turbulent, international biotechnology market. Having addressed the institutional financing gap at the start-up stage, it is not clear how the further support that these companies need to move into the later growth stages will materialise in Germany. These later, more costly, stages will be difficult to fund through government grants alone.

It is important to point out again here that it is arguably easier to target government funds towards the set of problems facing new start-ups than towards the more diverse, sub-sector-and strategy-specific issues that face more mature companies. For the latter, the government must obtain sufficient information to make sophisticated, firm-specific investments. Private services targeted at firms' specific requirements are probably needed. Investment banking, venture capital and public finance activities must expand in Germany if the hundreds of tiny start-ups now existing there are to develop.

Furthermore, the financial oversight and corporate governance of German biotechnology firms remains problematic. In addition to silent venture capital guaranteed by the federal government, substantial venture capital in Germany has been organised through 'innovation funds' administered by the banking sector, by regional public savings and investment banks in particular (Mietsch, 1999). Banks in insider-dominated corporate governance systems such as those in Germany tend to have excellent knowledge of particular firms, but usually do not have the detailed industry knowledge held by many venture capitalists that is necessary for investors wishing to channel money into higher-risk technologies (Tylecote and Conesa, 1999). The extensive involvement of public funds in the syndicates backing most new biotechnology firms limits the reservoir of experience the firm can draw upon through its venture capital partners. This could

Figure 5.3 **New venture capital investments in the UK and Germany, all sectors**

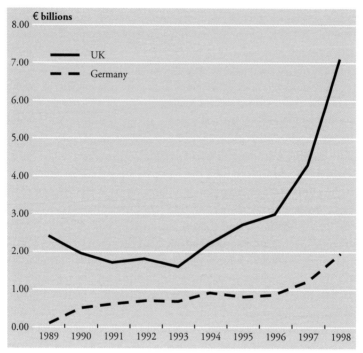

Source: BVK (1999b), 10.

be compounded by the relative immaturity of Germany's private venture capital sector. While several experienced venture capital houses in Germany do exist, those investing in biotechnology (and other young technology companies in other sectors) have only existed since 1997, starting up at the time when extensive governmental loans first became available (Mackewicz & Partner, 1998).

Total venture capital investments in all sectors in Germany more than doubled between 1996 and 1998 from €700 million to €1,900 million. This total represents only one-quarter of the venture capital invested in the UK (which in turn is less than 1 percent of that invested in the US). Venture capital investments in the UK also increased

Figure 5.4 **Venture capital investments in the biotechnology**
industry, 1994-1998

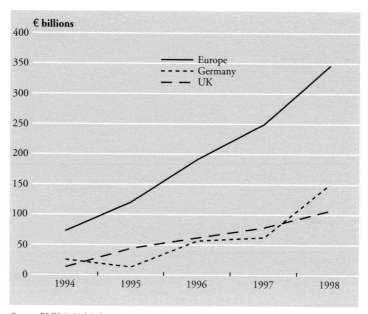

Source: BVK (1994-98).

significantly in the late 1990s, suggesting that international factors, and not only German policy reforms, may have contributed to the venture capital growth in Germany. See Figure 5.3.

The amount of venture capital invested in biotechnology specifically between 1994 and 1998 increased in Germany, the UK and the EU as a whole. German investments exceeded UK investments in 1998 (€148.34 million versus €113.07 million). Over the same time period, the share of total venture capital going to biotechnology has fluctuated considerably in Germany but the trend is generally positive. In the UK and the EU overall, by contrast, biotechnology's share of total venture capital has fallen since 1996. See Figures 5.4 and 5.5. In the next section we will investigate why, in the UK case, as total venture capital investments increased in the late 1990s, the amount

Figure 5.5 **Biotechnology investment as a proporation of total venture capital, 1994-1998**

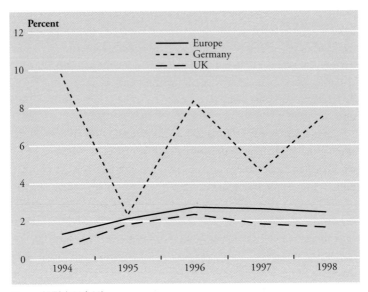

Source: BVK (1994-98).

invested in start-ups and company expansions has declined relative to that invested in buy-outs.

Public officials involved in the administration of federal subsidies, as well as officials of public banks, repeatedly stressed in our interviews that firm survival is their core focus. This may be a cause for concern. Understandably, public officials want to avoid large numbers of corporate failures. In addition to risking moderate sums of public money, the political backlash created by a large numbers of high-technology business failures could be embarrassing. To avoid this, controllers of public funds might channel them into lower-risk market segments and the public banks might be more reluctant to 'kill' funding for unsuccessful projects than private venture capitalists, who have a portfolio of investments spread across projects with different degrees of risk.

The venture capitalist tends to take a shorter-term view of investment than do public funders and will pull out of projects that look

likely to fail rather than risk losing more of their investors' money.
However, with their portfolio approach, the venture capitalist may be
more likely to support a risky project that seems to have good
prospects. So, even with public funds, a system is needed that supports
risk-taking investments but does not encourage propping up unprof-
itable projects. Without figures for investment by sector by public
funders, it is hard to assess the government's investment pattern. It is
also too early to know whether the government will step in with public money to bail out companies, that under strict competitive conditions would fail.

In addition, German financial markets for high-technology firms,
while growing, are still under-capitalised compared to those in the US
or the UK. The continued long-term uncertainty over a viable exit
option has limited the development of dedicated venture capital
financing, and especially so-called mezzanine financing, to fund the
expansion of start-up firms in preparation for going public[23]. While
the early success of the Neuer Markt has been a positive development,
the ability of investors to adopt successfully a portfolio approach when
investing in extremely high-risk start-ups is far from proven, as is the
reaction of German financial markets when, in the future, projects
begin to fail. It is not known whether this market will sustain industry downturns or what its reaction will be to the type of negative developments that have rocked the US and UK publicly-traded
biotechnology sectors in recent years.

5.3 Financial markets in the UK

In the corporate governance literature, economists tend to group the
UK and the US together. Both have diffuse and diversified ownership
structures, where the majority of large company shares are traded publicly. The strategic decisions of those public companies are therefore
pushed by shareholders looking for high and generally quick returns
(Blair, 1995; Dore, 1985). The ease with which investors can buy and

---

23 This opinion was expressed in interviews with German venture capitalists and
representatives of the tbg.

sell shares motivates riskier investment patterns on the part of private
and institutional investors than in the countries where exit options are
constrained. From the standpoint of venture capitalists, efficient capital markets provide them with exit options from their investments in
risky private technology companies.

Despite these general similarities, however, we find considerable
differences in the extent to which the financial systems of the UK and
US have worked to support biotechnology companies. In general,
investors in the UK seem more risk-averse compared with investors in
the US. This is reflected in the investment patterns of both venture
capitalists and public shareholders. In the biotechnology industry,
while US venture capitalists were quick to invest in new start-ups, UK
venture capitalists initially stayed away. Though policies have been
implemented by the UK government to improve the attractiveness of
high technology industry investments, the fact that 70 percent of new
UK venture capitalist investments in 1998 went into management
buy-outs (MBO) or management buy-ins (MBI) in 1998 shows that
deterrents remain (BVK, 1999b).

At the time of the founding of the UK's first biotechnology company, Celltech, in 1980, there were no UK venture capitalists with
biotechnology expertise that could support start-up companies.
Biotechnology Investment Limited (BIL), founded in 1981, and publicly quoted in 1984, was the first biotechnology industry targeted
group to raise a fund and provide support for companies in start-up
and emerging growth phases. According to an interview with its direc-
tor, Jeremy Curnock Cook (1999) '[In the 1980s], money was raised at
the fund (for early and later growth stages) because the UK markets at
the time were not sophisticated enough to know how to evaluate companies. Institutions relied on the fund to pick companies'. In a study
of the early UK biotechnology industry, Oakey et al. (1990) linked the
slow growth of the industry to venture capital organisations adopting a
hands-off level of involvement in the firms they funded and offering
investments only under highly regulated terms and conditions.

Initially, the lack of an exit option was also a major deterrent to
private investors in biotechnology in the UK. It was not until 1993
that the London Stock Exchange (LSE) allowed listings from compa-

nies without a track record established by three years of profits and at
least two products in clinical trials. No young biotechnology companies could meet these criteria. This meant that prior to 1993, at the
point where companies in the US would go public to raise money for
large, expensive clinical trials and for market launch, UK biotechnology companies had to seek additional rounds of scarce private finance.

The only exit option for the venture capitalist until 1993 was a
trade sale, i.e. finding a company buyer. The realisation gap in financing at the expansion stage quickly impacted on the earlier stages, creating an equity gap, as private investors were discouraged from
investing at all in the start-up companies. Data on the rate of start-up
development in the 1980s in the UK reflect the finance problems.
According to Senker (1996, 227), the rate of new firm creation was
slow and many of the companies were spun out of pharmaceutical
companies rather than started up by academics or other individuals.

Reforms in the early 1990s aimed to improve the situation. The
1993 amendment of Chapter 20 of the LSE rules enabled 'substantial
scientific research-based companies without an adequate trading record
to raise finance' and the establishment of the Alternative Investment
Market (AIM) in June 1995 improved biotechnology companies' access
to public equity. This improved access, in turn, helped to eliminate the
realisation gap. Easier exit options should attract venture capital and
other private investment to the earlier stages of development.

The amendment to chapter 20 of the LSE listing rules waived the
three-year trading history requirement for listing for 'companies primarily involved in the laboratory research and development of chemical and biological products or processes'. To be eligible, companies
provide evidence of support from 'sophisticated' investors, and of the
need for finance to bring products to a stage where they can generate
significant revenues. They must also have at least two drugs in clinical
trials. Despite this change, business consultants, such as Arthur
Andersen, still find the process for full listing to be difficult and time
consuming for biotechnology companies. The requirement that the
companies demonstrate *conclusively* that the products can generate significant revenues, is an especially difficult obstacle (Arthur Andersen,
1997).

Figure 5.6 **Venture capital investment by stage, 1998**

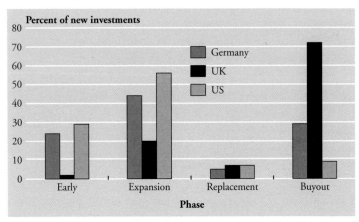

Note: The 'early' phase encompasses the seed and start-up phases that are listed separately for Germany and the UK but not for the US.

Sources: BVK (1999a,b).

AIM was set up to make public equity available to biotechnology companies even at very early stages. 'In principle, sophisticated management teams with access to good technology and a clear understanding of the commercialisation process can now access significant Stage One and Stage Two[24] public equity funding via AIM, without prior recourse to venture capital' (Arthur Andersen, 1997, 85). Arthur Andersen proposed that in the future, an early AIM listing would be a preferred option for second and third generation companies 'formed by or with biotechnology entrepreneurs who already have a track record of success' (ibid., 88). As of September 1999, few companies have taken this route to going public and the stock exchange faces real liquidity problems (Interview with J Curnock Cook, 1999)[25].

24 See Figure 3.8 for a description of the different finance stages.
25 In the last six months, the level of activity on AIM has increased and over eight AIM flotations are planned for the year 2000 (Clement, personal communication, May 2000).

Figure 5.7 **UK venture capital investment by stage, 1984 and**   **79**
1998

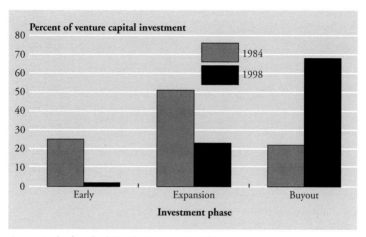

Sources: Bank of England (1996), 19; BVK (1999b).

The creation of new exit options did draw some venture capitalists towards the sector, though investments for early stage biotechnology (and all other industries) have remained scarce. Though it is the largest venture capital market in Europe (40 percent of Europe's venture capital is invested in the UK), almost three-quarters of the total is invested in MBO/MBIs with another fifth in expansions. In 1998, only 2 percent of the €7.1 million of venture capital went towards seed and start-up phases of companies. Figure 5.6 compares venture capital investment by phase for the US, Germany, and the UK.

The total amount of venture capital in Germany in 1998 (€1.9 million) was just 27 percent of that available in the UK. The amount invested in seed and early stage phases in the same year in Germany was 3.3 times that invested in the UK (€0.5 million versus €0.14 million respectively) (BVK, 1999b). For 1995, the European Venture Capitalist Association found that, in absolute terms, Germany, The Netherlands and Italy all invested more in the start-up and seed stages than did the UK (Bank of England, 1996, 21).

Figure 5.8a **US venture capital investment by stage, 1992-1998**

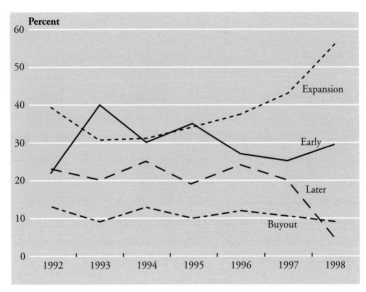

Source: BVK (1999a).

Between 1984 and 1998, more than 80 percent of the increase in total venture capital in the UK was invested in MBO/MBIs. Figure 5.7 shows how funds were shifted out of early and expansion stages into buyouts. A similar shift has not taken place in the US.

Figures 5.8a and 5.8b compare the investment stage shares of total venture capital in the US and the UK. The buyout share in the US has remained stable around 10 percent with an increasing share going towards company expansion.

Already noted earlier, a relatively small share (and absolute amount) of the venture capital has gone into UK biotechnology companies. It is striking that given the relative immaturity of the German venture capital industry that it invested more in its new biotechnology start-ups than did the venture capitalists in the UK. During the 1990s, venture capitalists in the US invested 75 percent, on average, in high tech sectors though the share going to biotechnology declined

Figure 5.8b **UK venture capital investment by stage, 1992-1998**

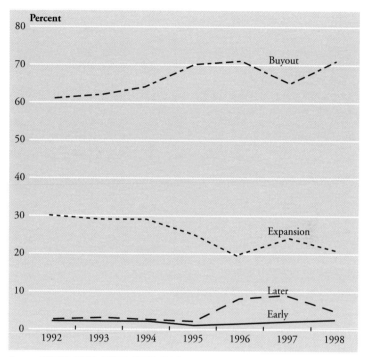

Sources: BVK (1999b); EVCA (1993-1998).

at the expense of computer and internet sectors. By contrast, UK venture capitalists invested only 25 percent, on average, in high tech sectors with about 2 percent going into biotechnology. See Table 5.4.

There are a number of possible reasons why UK venture capitalists remain relatively reluctant to invest in high-risk technology sectors in general and in biotechnology in particular. As was mentioned before, the risk profiles of funds' investors play a role. In the UK pension funds and insurance companies provide 61 percent of the venture capital. By comparison, banks have been the primary source of venture capital funding in Germany, Spain, France, and The Netherlands (Bank of England, 1996, 22). Though some debate exists, there is a

Table 5.4 **UK and US venture capital investment by industry,
1994-1998**

UK	1992	1993	1994	1995	1996	1997	1998
High-technology sub-total	12.1	22.2	14.1	23.6	18.4	30.6	24.9
Biotechnology	**0.8**	**1.8**	**0.6**	**1.8**	**2.3**	**5.2**	**1.6**
Medical/health related	3.5	6.1	3.9	8.1	4.8	7.1	3.9
Communications	4.5	1.7	1.6	4.6	3.8	3.6	10.7
Computers	2.1	8.4	4.8	5.3	4	10.4	6.3
Other electronics	1.2	4.2	3.2	3.8	3.5	4.3	2.4
Other (non high tech)	87.9	77.8	85.9	76.4	81.6	69.4	75.0
US	**1992**	**1993**	**1994**	**1995**	**1996**	**1997**	**1998**
High-technology sub-total	73.6	72.7	68.1	71.6	70.6	78.1	79.6
Biotechnology	**11.2**	**9.5**	**9.4**	**7.6**	**6.8**	**8.1**	**6.2**
Medical/health related	17.0	12.5	16.8	16.0	12.9	15.0	13.5
Communications	22.3	17.4	16.8	17.2	15.4	18.5	17.0
Computers	18.4	30.1	20.2	24.6	30.0	31.0	37.8
Other electronics	4.6	3.3	4.8	6.1	5.5	5.4	5.0
Other (non high tech)	26.4	27.3	31.9	28.4	29.4	21.9	20.4

Sources: BVK (1999a,b); EVCA (1993-1998).

general view that pension funds and insurance companies tend to have shorter time-horizons and are more risk averse than banks. In the US, there are two additional categories of investors involved in technology-based small firms that do not exist in the UK: foundations and endowment funds of universities and individual investors (21 percent and 12 percent of funds raised by venture capital firms in 1994 respectively) (ibid.). Both also tend to have longer time-horizons than do pension funds[26].

Biotechnology investments per deal tend to be small in scale (relative to the size of MBO/MBI deals for example), but require spe-

---

26 One correspondent suggested that a reason for the UK focus in MBO/MBIs is the dominance in this venture capital market of large private equity players who have problems allocating their sizeable funds (billions of £) at the early stage. These types of investments involve relatively small amounts of money but require a lot of supervision (Clement, personal communication, May 2000).

cialised technology experts and close supervision and monitoring. The   **83**
UK funds lack sufficient numbers of industry experts and are perhaps
too small to afford to specialise in these high-risk sectors (Bank of
England, 1996).

A lack of success stories, coupled with recent disappointments in
the largest UK public biotechnology companies, means that it has also
become difficult to raise money through an IPO. Figure 5.9 compares
the two-year relative performance of stocks for the biotechnology sectors in Europe, the US, and the UK for the August 1996-July 1998
period. While the continental European and US indexes are fairly flat
in early 1998, the UK index declines dramatically. As reported by
Ernst & Young: 'Highly publicised events at Biocompatibles
International plc, British Biotech, Cortecs and Scotia Holdings, which
saw the departures of CEOs, had a negative impact on shareholder
confidence in those companies and consequently the sector. As these
were four of the seven largest European entrepreneurial life-science
companies (ELISCOs) at the start of the year, their share performance
had a dramatic impact on the sector's overall performance, accounting
for 97 percent of the sector's decline' (Ernst & Young, 1999, 42). See
Figure 5.9. Revived investor opinion (at least temporarily) in late
1999 and early 2000 may mean increased financial opportunities for
biotechnology companies in the future.

But even as the UK biotechnology index recovered, sector analysts
remained only cautiously optimistic. They view the recent M&A
activity as positive but remain pessimistic about the returns from
products currently in late stage development. 'It remains a fact that we
have not seen a blockbuster drug emerge from the UK sector and the
near-term pipeline does not look inspiring. The aforementioned rally
in US biotechnology stocks has been driven by the launch of a few
blockbusters followed by a stream of successful products. A similar
product stream is required in Europe to truly deliver the biotechnology promise in the eyes of investors' (Warburg Dillon Read, 2000a, 15).

If companies must delay going public until later in their products'
clinical trials process (when they are perceived as a better investment),
then they are faced with the task of financing those expensive clinical
trials through private means. One possibility is to try and do more

Figure 5.9 **Relative performance of continental European, UK and US biotechnology stock indexes, August 1996-July 1998**

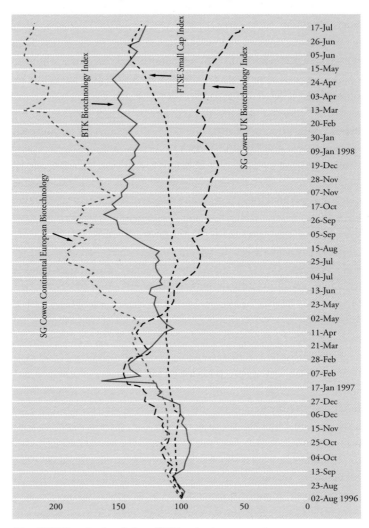

Notes: BTK Biotechnology Index = US biotechnology companies.
FTSE Small Cap Index shows how UK biotechnology companies performed relative to other small capitalisation companies over the same time period.

Source: SG Cowen (1998).

deals with major pharmaceutical companies, but these large compa- **85**
nies are becoming more selective and are also waiting until more clinical evidence is available before licensing-in biotechnology products.
Industry analysts are pushing biotechnology-biotechnology mergers
and consolidation as a way to make companies more attractive to both
private and public investors. Larger, consolidated companies would be
able to present a broader product portfolio, and to draw upon a more
comprehensive set of human resources and experiences.

A number of policies have been proposed with the aim of improving the funding situation for early stage, high technology industries.
These include capital gains tax reform, the creation of venture capital
trusts, and enterprise investment schemes to attract more individual
and institutional investors. UK companies do not have access to the
kind of public seed money available in Germany, and communication
between companies and existing business angels could be improved.
Tax incentives will not overcome this information gap.

Having expert managers from the start is essential, preferably managers with experience in the industry, in starting-up companies, and in
arranging alliances with major pharmaceutical firms. The next section
therefore looks at the market for such managers in UK and Germany.

6 LABOUR MARKETS FOR SCIENTISTS AND MANAGERS

6.1 Staffing companies – the issue

Attracting and retaining staff and managers to work in the highly risky and dynamic environments of biotechnology start-ups is the third challenge we investigate. For a start-up to succeed, the scientific discoveries of researchers must be brought together with the commercial expertise of experienced managers and venture capitalists that can sell discoveries to potential finance providers and buyers.

For venture capitalists, business proposals backed by experienced management and a strong patent position are the most attractive (Ernst & Young, 1999). Ideally, these managers would have experience both with start-ups and with the industry. This means understanding the science as well as the expectations of major pharmaceutical companies (future potential customers or alliance partners) and venture capitalists. The problem is that traditionally, university-trained scientists have little or no commercial experience and lack the objectivity to assess the commercial prospects of their research over the development stages. So, in the short term, the start-up team must attract managers from outside. In the longer term, in-house training and learning by doing can improve the scientists' commercial skills.

This chapter focuses primarily on the ability of biotechnology firms to attract and motivate scientists and managers, in particular during the early stages of the firm's development. We concentrate on three areas: 1. the firm's establishment of links with star scientists; 2. its ability to find and retain staff within the context of a volatile, high-risk industry; and 3. its ability to provide adequate performance incentives within a complex, high-pressure work environment.

a) Establishing links with star scientists
Zucker et al. (1994, 1998) and Zucker and Darby (1999) have created a substantial database that has been used to link the probable success of biotechnology firms with their access to star scientists in applicable fields of molecular biology. Elite or star scientists are defined in terms of their research productivity: 'those discovering more than 40 genetic sequences and/or authoring 20 or more articles report-

ing such discoveries up to April 1990' (Zucker and Darby, 1999, 120).   **87**
They found 327 stars world-wide – less than 0.8 percent of all authors
in GenBank but accounting for 17.3 percent of all the articles in that
database (ibid., 121).

In a search for links between citations of star scientists and specific private biotechnology firms, Zucker and Darby (1999, 121) found
for the period 1976-1990 that 'for the average firm, five articles co-
authored by an academic star and the firm's key scientist result in
about five more products in development, 3.5 more products on the
market, and 860 more employees'. In general, star scientists are linked
with a number of key competencies needed by biotechnology firms
that include: access to cutting edge research methods and intellectual
property; a strong reputation that can be used to attract venture capital; and highly qualified staff.

Zucker and Darby's arguments seem especially convincing for firms
working in market segments characterised by intense research races to
patent compounds, where tight on-going links with key scientists are
important. Their analysis has not been updated; however, to examine
the importance of star scientist links in other emerging market niches,
particularly in more applied areas such as platform technologies.

In the therapeutics segments where star scientists have been found
to be important, national level institutions must address two challenges. The first problem is to support a sufficient science base. For
the 1976-1990 period, the Zucker and Darby data show that the UK
and Germany were far behind the US in generating star scientists.
Furthermore, these data suggest that many key European scientists
(some 25 percent of the Europe-born star scientists) migrated to the
US for training and were more likely to have maintained strong links
with the science/business complex there, rather than in Europe.
Second, as discussed in Section 4, technology transfer rules influence
a country's scientists' decisions about whether, how, when and where
to participate in the private sector. Scientists need clear incentives and
channels to collaborate with the commercial biotechnology sector.

b) Access to high-quality managers and scientific personnel

Many biotechnology start-ups, especially within the therapeutics market segment, fail and enter into bankruptcy or are sold to other firms. In companies that do survive, the set of competencies they need changes rapidly as companies move through the growth lifecycle, taking products into new development stages, killing failing projects, and starting new ones. In addition, as was discussed in Section 3 (and is argued by Powell, 1996, Penan, 1996, and others), biotechnology is a network based industry. Innovation is dependent on the flow of knowledge and staff between university laboratories, start-up research firms, and large pharmaceutical firms. Collaborative projects, strategic alliances and so forth facilitate this exchange of knowledge, as does the movement of scientists and technicians between firms.

In biotechnology, the ability to quickly hire new scientists or managers – and at times to fire others – becomes an important organisational issue. Firms must be able to reconstitute quickly the structure of their research competencies as they move into different stages of the development cycle or move in and out of different research fields. To do this, they must have access to a pool of scientists, technicians, and other specialists with known reputations in particular areas who can be recruited quickly to work on research projects. Co-ordination mechanisms to recycle human resources across regional networks of public and private research laboratories must be developed[27].

Labour market institutions, employment practices within large firms, and laws governing the activities of scientists within public research organisations all influence the mobility of managers and scientists. If asset recycling is difficult or if there is a cultural stigma attached to failing or changing jobs regularly, then specialists and managers may choose to avoid firms with high-risk research projects, fearing a negative sigma from an association with failed projects. Similarly, if career mobility across firms and non-profit research laboratories is not supported within a country's labour market structures, then the rapid transfer of knowledge across public institutions and firms driving innovative research clusters will be difficult to sustain.

---

27 See Saxenian (1994) and Bahrami and Evans (1995) for an elaboration of this argument within the context of labor market dynamics within Silicon Valley in California, US.

c) Organising high-powered incentives

To obtain and retain the necessary human and financial resources, companies must create the organisational structures necessary for innovation. Companies face problems motivating staff to commit to what are often demanding, competitive and time-intensive work environments and to contribute their knowledge and abilities to the research team. Organisational economists refer to the latter as hold-up risks. Scientists may have private incentives (regarding accreditation for key discoveries, or over financial rewards) that disrupt team research because they are reluctant to share their highly specialised knowledge with the other researchers in the firm[28].

Biotechnology firms often employ performance-based incentive schemes to induce employees to commit to intense work environments and reduce hold-up risks. A team's performance, rather than an individual's, may be the focus of evaluation. Over the last decade, companies have primarily used share-options packages. Staffs accept these packages in the expectation that their company will be one of the few whose share value multiplies when it goes public. Some authors have argued that it is the prospect of large financial rewards that aligns the private incentives of scientists with those of commercial managers (Miller, 1992; Simpson, 1998). Another common approach to incentivise work is to allow scientists to share the limelight generated by important discoveries by encouraging them to publish important results in high-profile scientific journals.

National rules strongly influence the incentive instruments the owners and top management of firms can offer employees. This is particularly true for stock option packages. In addition to different taxation practices on capital gains and salaries, Germany and the UK have different company laws regarding employee representation rights. Combined with the existence of cultural norms that shun failure, these laws have created obstacles towards the use of direct, high-powered, financial incentives within both countries, but especially in Germany.

28 See Milgrom and Roberts (1992) and Werth (1994) for examples from a prominent US biotechnology company.

6.2 Labour market structures in Germany

Literature has focused in particular on the star scientist problem in Germany (Momma and Sharp, 1999). According to Zucker and Darby's data from the 1980s, only 5.7 percent of the world's star scientists (24 of 417) worked in Germany, and none had links with new biotechnology firms in Germany[29] (compared to direct firm linkages for 33 percent of star scientists in the US)[30]. This finding is not surprising, since virtually no dedicated biotechnology firms existed in Germany during the period of Zucker and Darby's study. As outlined in the technology section, intellectual property and employment rules in Germany created constraints on university professors who sought to establish a relationship with a dedicated biotechnology firm, particularly during the initial, spin-off phase from university research. Recent experience shows that these rules can be somewhat malleable. In the last few years some prominent German scientists have started to set up collaborations with biotechnology firms in Germany.

The star scientist issue aside, we found that labour market institutions, labour and company laws and the employment practices of large firms, continue to create important obstacles for entrepreneurial firms attempting to use high-powered incentives within high-risk technology companies in Germany.

Until recently, many German employees expected to spend their entire careers at the same firm where they completed their formal postgraduate apprenticeship (or, in the case of engineers and scientists, an internship arranged in conjunction with their university degree) (see Lehrer, 1997; Vitols et al., 1997; Abramson et al., 1997). Long-term employment is strongly influenced by codetermination rights granted to employees of most firms under German labour laws (see

29 A star is said to be linked to a biotechnology firm if, while listing a university or research institute in the same country as the firm, he or she has ever co-authored with a scientist who listed the firm as his or her affiliation on that article (Zucker and Darby, 1999, 121).

30 Many German scientists work in the biotechnology industry in the US but they are included in the US numbers.

Katzenstein, 1987: 125-147 for an overview). Employees in any German firm with more than five workers have the legal right to form a works council. Works councils have consultation rights over many areas of work organisation and training, and a formal veto right to proposals for overtime work. While there exist no formal laws stipulating long-term employment, German labour has historically used its power on supervisory boards within large public firms, as well as its formal consultative rights within works councils, to demand unlimited employment contracts (Streeck, 1984).

German codetermination appears to be spreading into the new entrepreneurial sector. A recent survey by the *Deutsche Börse*, for example, found that about 20 percent of the leading *Neuer Markt* firms had already established works councils, while most other firms had instituted less formal consultation committees between skilled workers and management (*Wirtschaftswoche*, 2000).

Codetermination practices make it difficult for firms to fire individual employees as part of the normal course of business, though it is possible to sell off subsidiaries and business units and use early retirement schemes to cut labour costs[31]. While it is easier to fire salaried managers, large firms have often developed long-term employment practices with regard to management as well (Lehrer, 1997; Monks and Minow, 1995, 287-295). Recent moves by major pharmaceutical companies to downsize upper management suggest that there may be more room for flexibility at these levels but, in general, the practice of long-term employment tends to be the norm for skilled workers.

The German industrial relations system also influences the design of performance incentives. There is evidence in the literature to show that for large firms, long-term employment and codetermination rights for employees motivate management to seek broad consensus across the firm when making major decisions (Vitols et al., 1997). Because unilateral decision-making is limited, it is difficult for German firms to create strong performance incentives for individual

---

31 See Becker et al. (1999) for a discussion of recent downsizing difficulties at Hoechst, for example.

managers. Representatives of works councils and mid-level management committees have traditionally shunned the use of individual performance incentives, arguing that employees should be rewarded on a collective rather than an individual basis (Lehrer, 1997). Though works councils cannot prevent management from employing individual performance evaluations, their statutory consultation rights over key aspects of company personnel policy lend leverage to works council demands. As a result, performance rewards tend to be targeted at groups rather than individuals, and individual performance assessments and bonus schemes are limited.

Potential entrepreneurs have also faced a variety of tax and cultural disincentives. Until early 1998 German finance law placed restrictions on companies trading in their own shares, making it difficult for firms to issue stock options to employees. Furthermore, an extremely high – 60 percent – capital gains tax has to be paid on the sale of large share-holdings[32].

Cultural factors are more difficult to quantify. Chief executives interviewed agreed, however, that the German business community tends to shun failure, in part through the expectation that owners and managers of firms should provide long-term security to employees and investors. As a result, the ability of entrepreneurs to learn from the experience of failed projects is limited in Germany. As an article on European entrepreneurs summed up the situation 'If you start a company in London or Paris and go bust, you have just ruined your future. Do it in Silicon Valley and you have just completed your entrepreneurial training' (*The Economist*, 1997).

Starting in the mid-1990s, and especially in 1997 with the formation of the Neuer Markt, important changes have taken place in Germany that affect entrepreneurial company ability to attract management and staff. The development of a German equity market for

32 Until 1998, a large share-holding was anything exceeding a 25 percent stake. The new SPD-Green coalition government has lowered that floor to 10 percent. In February 2000, Chancellor Schroeder's cabinet approved a tax reform plan that would reduce corporate taxes from 40 percent to 25 percent and eliminate the 60 percent tax on selling large share holdings from other companies (*New York Times*, February 10, 2000).

technology firms, coupled with a March 1998 financial reform to   **93**
legalise stock options, have made it easier for firms to offer stock
option plans to their employees. The owners and managers of several
German biotechnology firms we interviewed claimed that younger
Germans are increasingly willing to work within riskier entrepreneurial firms in order to obtain positions of responsibility earlier in their
careers, driven by the hope of increased wealth through share option
schemes. Biotechnology companies tend to hire younger people and
that makes it easier for owner-entrepreneurs to gain a consensus in
favour of individual performance assessments and incentives. Of the
many young German biotechnology firms we visited in 1999, none
had formed works councils and most had implemented, or had plans
to implement, stock option schemes.

The strength, during 1998 and 1999, of the Neuer Markt, combined with the general upsurge of activity within the German biotechnology sector, have made stock options a realistic incentive device.
Many companies are using share options to reward end-of-the-year
good performance as well. A strong, small-firm-friendly, domestic
stock market also makes the prospect of going public in the near future
more feasible for many companies. According to Schitag Ernst &
Young's 1998 German biotechnology survey, some 80 percent of small
German life science companies list an IPO as a preferred way forward.
The persistence of high taxes on exercised stock options remains a serious problem, however (Schitag Ernst & Young, 1998). Tax reform
proposals for the Budget 2000 include changes to capital gains and
corporate tax structures (*New York Times*, February 10, 2000).

While the ability to provide staff with attractive performance
incentives has improved, most German technology firms continue to
face obstacles in obtaining high quality management and scientists.
Because labour markets for mid-career managerial and scientific expertise are relatively underdeveloped in Germany, the flexible labour market mechanisms needed for many biotechnology firms to compete
successfully in technology races over the medium to long term do not
exist. The career damaging risk of leaving an established large company or prestigious university professorship to start a new firm remains
high relative to the potential gains of doing so. More success stories

are needed to motivate these types of career shifts. The lack of experienced managers and scientists willing to work within entrepreneurial start-ups to set a precedent, is seen as the key constraint on the further enlargement of the German biotechnology industry (*The Economist*, 1998; Schitag Ernst & Young, 1998).

Finally, the star scientist problem in Germany appears now to be lessening, although still problematic. As Zucker and Darby's dataset has yet to be extended into the 1990s, comprehensive trends are not available. However, data compiled by Momma and Sharp (1999, 270-271) suggest that the overall standing of German universities and public research institutes in the life sciences has improved substantially. According to these figures, 18 percent of the top-class universities in the mid-1990s were German, compared to 44 percent in the US and 16 percent in the UK. Furthermore, there are some prominent cases of star scientists developing affiliations with German biotechnology companies. Perhaps best known is the alliance between Nobel Prize winner Professor Christiane Nuesslein-Volhard of the Max Planck Institute and Artemis, a functional genomics company formed in part to commercialise her research. Laboratories involved with internationally recognised research programmes, in particular the Human Genome Project, have also become closely involved with new spin-off companies. Perhaps the most prominent example here is the Genome Pharmaceutical Corporation in Munich, which is making use of sequencing technology developed at the Max Planck Institute for Genetics in Berlin.

However, our interviews have suggested that relationships between university scientists and dedicated biotechnology firms in Germany still differ from those in the US. Relationships in Germany are more of the professional consultant type. As noted in Section 4, German civil service laws make it difficult for university professors to take leaves of absence or sabbaticals to work intensively in a private sector research laboratory, a practice commonly associated with US biotechnology (Kenney, 1986). Overall, while large numbers of German university professors have developed consulting relationships with Germany's new biotechnology firms or serve on scientific advisory boards, as of late 1998 no professor had been enticed to leave his or

her university chair to work full-time within a dedicated biotechnolo- **95**
gy firm. The primary source of employees (and entrepreneurs) for
Germany's new biotechnology firms have been PhD students and
postdoctoral researchers from German biomedical university laboratories who face poor employment prospects within German universities.

6.3 Labour market structures in the UK

The UK has labour and company laws that are more conducive to the
development of the labour markets and employee motivational
schemes suitable for entrepreneurial biotechnology firms. Labour markets are relatively deregulated and open, while company law imposes
few restrictions on owners and top managers in creating performance-
based incentive systems. In each of the areas discussed here – star scientist linkages, employee incentives, and labour market mobility – the
UK has developed scientific practices, financial incentive systems, and
labour market institutions that are closer to the US model than in
Germany. After outlining these structures we turn to the puzzling
question of why, despite a seemingly favourable institutional climate,
problems remain in the staff and management area for UK biotechnology firms.

In the UK there exists a flexible market for managers and technical employees, and poaching between companies is common practice
(Charkham, 1995; Lehrer, 1997; Vitols et al., 1997). This makes the
long-term employment contracts with low-powered performance
incentives, which tend to predominate within large German firms, less
viable. Furthermore, the top managers of firms have more flexibility
over internal labour market policy. German-style works councils have
no statutory organisational rights or consultation powers in the UK.
If particular research units are not meeting expected performance stan-
dards or, due to a change in strategy, are no longer needed, they may
simply be cut. While, in practice, many middle managers and
researchers may work with one firm throughout their careers, there are
generally no long-term employment guarantees. This creates the
opportunity for top management to cut non-performing assets quickly and replace them with new groups of employees hired on the open

labour market or rapidly from another part of the firm.

If employment contracts can be limited in duration and there is an open market for valued scientific and managerial skills, it follows that strong incentives must be designed in order to foster loyalty to the firm. In the UK corporate governance environment, higher wages are part of a broader incentive structure to reward superior individual performance. Within large UK firms, top management has wide latitude in crafting incentive systems, primarily through bonuses tied to yearly performance reviews and a variety of stock option plans. An additional incentive common in large UK firms is the opportunity for rapid advancement through firm hierarchies and the granting of unilateral decision-making power to key employees (Lehrer, 1997).

The existence of flexible labour market policies and strongly incentivized career patterns within the large-firm sector should actively complement the strategies of smaller entrepreneurial firms. This is particularly important in the labour market area: if large firms hire and fire, this generates pools of experienced scientists and managers that smaller firms can draw upon. Compared with the German system, the institutional structure of UK labour markets seems to facilitate the construction of biotechnology company strategies that can easily move human resources in and out, reflecting changes in the firms' needs. A similar analysis holds with regard to stock options and other incentive plans. The widespread use of incentive plans and individually oriented performance reviews within large firms creates legitimacy and know-how for the introduction of similar schemes within smaller firms.

Despite the problems discussed earlier in the financial area, the UK still has the most developed equity markets in Europe in terms of market capitalisation, and remains the only market to have successfully promoted IPOs for several dozen biotechnology firms, some 40 of which are listed on UK stock exchanges. Stocks as performance incentives are thus embedded in highly credible financial market institutions.

Finally, as discussed in the technology section, the structure of the UK university-system should create adequate incentives for scientists to make linkages with the private biotechnology sector. The legal civil

service and administrative requirements seen to inhibit active collabo-   **97**
ration between professors and technology firms in Germany do not
exist in the UK. Technology transfer and intellectual property laws
governing university research should align incentives between university administrators and professors regarding the commercialisation of
research. In general, the institutional incentives facing professors have
largely converged with those in the US (Senker, 1996).

Overall, institutions structuring UK labour market practices and
company organisation combine with the strategies of larger firms to
create an environment that should be conducive to entrepreneurial
firms having adequate management, staff, and links to university scientists. Nevertheless a consistent theme in our UK interviews, confirmed also by Ernst & Young (1999) and the government report on
cluster development (Sainsbury et al., 1999), is that recruiting high
quality staff remains an important problem in the UK biotechnology
industry. We do not have a definitive answer for why this is problem
persists, but suggest three factors that may contribute to them.

First, the overall size of the UK labour market for scientists might
not be sufficient. Unfortunately no comparative data linking the
desired versus actual size of labour markets for scientists, technicians,
or management exist for the life-sciences area. However, some cir-
cumstantial evidence suggests this might be a problem. The Zucker
and Darby (1999, 120) data show a small but significant emigration
of star scientists from European countries, including the UK, to the
US. Moreover, interviews with head-hunters, venture capitalists, and
managers of biotechnology companies have confirmed a generally held
assumption that large numbers of mid-level British scientists and managers within the life sciences area have taken jobs in the US. While
higher base salaries are a crucial factor, so too is the ability of the US
sector to generate large numbers of successful firms, at least in the
medium-term, through IPOs, which makes stock-options and other
performance incentives more attractive in the US.

Second, critics have charged that the UK government has not
invested sufficiently in basic research. Increased investments could
increase the number of star scientists operating in the UK, and would
increase the general size of the life-sciences labour market. The sup-

ply-side support of life-science research is clearly important, but more data are needed to establish whether insufficient investment has been made into the UK science base. According to the star scientist data from 1990, the UK is as far behind the US as Germany (some 30 UK stars, about 7 percent of the global total). Momma and Sharp's data from the mid-1990s, on the other hand, show a substantial improvement in the general ranking of UK life science research, which emerged as Europe's leader.

Finally, cultural factors, particularly among managers, comprise another possible problem. Several of our interview partners believed that top UK managers are more risk averse than in the US, preferring to work within large companies rather than in risky start-ups. While cultural factors can clearly be important and long lasting, in this case an explanation could also include incentives created by the generally world-class performance of the UK's leading pharmaceutical firms, compared to the mediocre recent performance of the small-firm biotechnology sector. Especially over the last two years, when the UK biotechnology index has plummeted, stock options and other normally high-powered performance incentives within the small-firm sector have become devalued. While a 'chicken and egg' problem might exist here - the performance of the UK biotechnology sector might improve if more top UK life-science managers took jobs in entrepreneurial firms - this problem speaks in general of the need for clear success stories to emerge from the UK sector.

7 CONCLUSION AND POLICY IMPLICATIONS

The US is the only country with a critical mass of successful biotechnology companies, i.e. companies earning profits through sales of products approved for market or through research and license deals with other companies. Striving to follow the US's lead, many European countries have introduced industry-specific policies to foster the commercialization of their own biomedical research.

Through a comparison of the UK and German industries, we have argued in this report that any policy package to promote the biotechnology industry must respond to a set of industry-specific demands but must also be tailored to reflect specific national institutions. Given differences in the key institutions that support the industry – university technology transfer systems, high-risk finance, and the labour markets for entrepreneurial scientists and managers – the sub-sector areas focused on and the strategies that companies use to compete with may also be quite different between countries.

Our report highlights a number of key findings. Firstly, we have identified important differences in the structure and performance of the German and UK industries. The German industry is relatively young. As of late 1998, 60 percent of its companies were less than two years old and over 80 percent had fewer than 50 employees. Thus most of the German biotechnology companies are still in the start-up stage. In terms of sub-market specialisation, more than half of German firms focus on platform technologies and diagnostics.

By contrast, the UK industry is more mature. In 1998, more than 80 percent of its companies were more than five years old. The range of sub-market sectors represented is also broader. One third of biotechnology companies are undertaking research in new therapeutics. The rest are spread between technologies, services, and diagnostics. There are many more public companies in the UK – close to 50 versus five in Germany – but as of May 2000 only one UK company had successfully launched a UK-developed therapeutic onto the market[33].

---

33 The UK does have many more products in late clinical trials and pending market approval.

100

Secondly, using information about the industry's dynamics in the UK, Germany, and the US we have identified three key competencies that companies must have in order to innovate and grow:

1. the ability to access and commercialize new technology;
2. the ability to access sufficient finance; and,
3. the ability to recruit and retain capable and experienced research scientists and managers.

The date of entry into the industry potentially impacts a company's choice of competitive strategies and market segments. Because Germany entered the industry relatively late, therefore, one might expect to find a different profile of market segments and strategic trajectories. Advancements in technology and changes in the expectations and priorities of finance providers mean than different product strategies and business models are called for in the year 2000 than in 1980. However, we argue that the differences between the UK and German industries are also linked to differences in the two countries' respective national institutions that support these key competencies.

Third, our research of Germany and the UK suggests that government policy plays a role in shaping a country's industry development. The mere fact that Germany has gone from having virtually no companies in 1990 to having more than 200 ten years later certainly supports this view. Clearly countries can learn from each other's experiences. However, we caution against attempts to directly transfer or borrow policies from one country to another, especially when the countries involved have highly dissimilar institutional structures, as in the case of the UK and Germany. Most broadly, government policies must be incentive-compatible with the orientation of long-established institutional frameworks governing the economy.

Turning to the country cases. The German technology policy was largely designed to circumvent long-standing institutional obstacles that deterred the development of high-technology industries. Because markets for entrepreneurial scientists and for venture capital were underdeveloped, institutional frameworks had to be created from scratch. With German industry in its infancy, policies have been concentrated on providing start-up capital and on orchestrating linkages between university research and technology transfer centres, venture **101** capitalists, and new start-ups. Regional support infrastructures have also been developed such as incubator laboratories, the training and recruitment of local experts in patent law, and provision of business development planning and other services.

In the case of finance, venture capital and equity markets in Germany are relatively underdeveloped (or at least inexperienced) when compared with those in the UK and US[34]. As a result, public money and lower-risk bank finance is backing many of the start-up projects. To secure future funds under such conditions, companies are encouraged to pursue platform technology strategies that are perhaps less risky and certainly take less time to develop and market than new therapeutics.

From the standpoint of labour, norms which deter quick hires and fires, and poor incentives for risk-taking career moves, make it difficult for German firms to change research trajectories quickly, for example by closing down some facilities altogether. This, combined with the generally tight German labour markets for experienced managers and technicians in biotechnology, may also encourage firms to choose the platform technology area. In addition to the lower financial risks involved, if core technologies in this area are more stable, long-term human resource commitments should be easier to sustain.

In the future, German policy might have to become more diffuse to respond to the more diversified needs of growing companies in a range of product segments. An important question is whether markets for high-risk equity capital and experienced scientists and managers will evolve to meet the demands of a growing mass of companies. Until now, the government has stepped in to provide start-up funding and make sector-specific exemptions from various labour and tax laws. What is unclear is whether wider institutional and regulatory reforms will be required for the industry to flourish.

Another important issue concerns the focus of German biotechnology firms on platform technologies. Though difficult to prove

34 Significant capital gains tax breaks have served as a significant incentive to attract individual investors into the biotechnology and other high technology industries.

conclusively, due to the immaturity of the German sector, it seems that the incentives shaped by the German institutional environment have helped create this pattern of specialisation. A question worth further research is whether Germany will continue along this fairly specialized industry trajectory exploiting institutional advantages in this area. Is this a sustainable position or does success in the biotechnology industry depend ultimately on companies diversifying into a broader spectrum of business strategies? Recent analyst reports point to a decline in public and private investor and major pharma interest and need for strict technology providers (SG Cowen, 2000a; Ernst & Young, 2000). If this were the case, what institutional changes would have to take place to facilitate this kind of evolution in Germany?

The UK presents additional challenges for analysis. Using the US as a basis for comparison, the UK has developed broadly similar institutions to support high-risk, therapeutics-dominated corporate strategies, and in fact was able to develop Europe's first and largest biotechnology industry. However, over the past couple of years, the industry has stalled and a critical mass of successful UK biotechnology companies has not developed. Clinical trials for a few lead products produced disappointing results and key companies have had problems recruiting and keeping experienced managers. Markets have responded positively to recent mergers and to news about product developments but new companies continue to report difficulties securing sufficient venture capital to bridge the gap between the early start-up stage and an IPO.

Our research points to a number of weaknesses in the UK incentive network. Many have also been identified in the DTI's (1999) *Genome Valley Report*. Key shortages of both finance and expertise appear to exist within university technology transfer offices. While a vibrant venture capital community does exist, with access to mature capital markets, the bulk of venture capital has, in recent years, been channeled into safer investments promising quicker returns, such as MBOs and MBIs. Finally, with regard to managers, although labour markets are largely deregulated and firms can deploy the high-powered motivational structures needed to compete in intense innovation races, there nevertheless appear to be shortages of talented scientists

and managers willing to work within promising UK biotechnology   **103**
firms. As with venture capital, risk aversion could be a factor, while
others suggest that many top UK researchers have relocated to the US
(Sainsbury et al., 1999).

Policy makers in the UK have focused on cluster policy as a tool
with which to try and remedy some of these problems. Cluster policies aim to facilitate or subsidise the construction of linkages between
university biomedical research centres and surrounding communities
of biotechnology firms and private sector support firms, such as patent
lawyers, venture capitalists, and business consultants. These initiatives
presume that the key problem facing the UK industry is one of coordination. This means that the key components of the network exist in
the UK, but lack adequate incentives needed to work together. Our
research, however, suggests that key problems facing the UK also lie in
the area of supply. Especially in the areas of finance and management
there are simply not enough experts working within the small firm
high-technology sector. Supply-related factors are not addressed by
cluster policy.

One way to alleviate shortages may be industry consolidation. This
would reduce the number of firms competing for finance, managers,
and high-quality scientists and technicians. Through broadening
product and technology portfolios and widening the firm's skill assets,
it is likely that the quality of a firm's projects would improve, leading
to a better prospect of finding alliances with large pharmaceutical
firms, which could lead to more interest from the investment community, and so on. This logic motivated Celltech's takeover of
Chiroscience in August 1999 (and this new group to acquire Medeva
in November 1999). An interesting question is whether by promoting
consolidation and the development of larger companies, one risks
undermining the innovative process driven by small focused
entrepreneurial firms.

A final and most critical area of supply concerns the science base.
Common wisdom within high-technology industry is that a large proportion of managers and especially venture capitalists were first trained
as research scientists. More public resources to boost the development
of high quality scientists may be needed both to generate research that

can be transferred to the private sector, and to produce a sufficient number of managers and venture capitalists with the technical expertise needed to select and steer projects to the market. The problems facing the UK biotechnology sector might therefore be ones of scale, i.e. of producing a sufficiently large and high quality science base to generate the needed scientific *and* managerial expertise.

REFERENCES

Abramson N, Encarnação J, Reid P and Schmoch U, eds. (1997) **105**
Technology Transfer Systems in the United States and Germany. Washington,
D.C.: National Academy Press.

Adelberger K (forthcoming) 'A developmental German state? Explaining
growth in German biotechnology and venture capital.' *German Politics.*

Albert (1993) *Capitalism vs Capitalism: How America's Obsession with
Individual Achievement and Short-Term Profit Has Led it to the Brink of
Collapse.* New York: Four Walls Eight Windows.

Arora A and Gambardella A (1990) 'Complementary and External
Linkages: The Strategies of the Large Firms in Biotechnology.' *The Journal
of Industrial Economics*, Vol. 38, No. 4, June, 361-379.

Arthur Andersen (1994) *UK Biotech '94 – The Way Ahead.* UK: Arthur
Andersen; Andersen Worldwide, SC.

Arthur Andersen (1997) *UK Biotech '97 – Making the Right Moves.* UK:
Arthur Andersen; Andersen Worldwide, SC.

Arthur Andersen (1998) *Technology Transfer in the UK Life Sciences.* UK:
Arthur Andersen/Garrets/Dundas & Wilson.

Arthur Andersen (2000) *UK Life Sciences Report.* UK: Arthur Andersen;
Andersen Worldwide, SC.

Ashton, G (forthcoming) 'Trends in the Development of Pharmaceutical
Products of Biotechnology', PhD dissertation in progress.

Bahrami H and Evans S (1995) 'Flexible Re-cycling and High-Technology
Entrepreneurship.' *California Management Review*, Vol. 37, No. 3, Spring,
62-88.

Bank of England (1996) *The Financing of Technology-Based Small Firms.*
London: Bank of England.

Barley S, Freeman J and Hybels R (1994) 'Strategic Alliances in
Commercial Biotechnology', in Nohria N and Eccles R eds. *Networks and
Organisations: Structure, Form and Action.* Boston: Harvard Business
School Press, 311-347.

Barnett R et al. (1998) *Biotechnology in Germany – Report of an ITS Expert
Mission.* Bonn: British Embassy.

106   Becker S, Menz W and Sablowski R (1999) 'Ins Netz gegangen: Industrielle Beziehungen im Netzwerk-Konzern am Beispiel der Hoechst AG.' *Industrielle Beziehungen* 6 (1), 8-35.

BIA (1999a) *Industrial Markets for UK Biotechnology – Trends and Issues.* London: BioIndustry Association.

BIA (1999b) *Mission to the US.* London: BioIndustry Association.

BIO (1999a) *Guide to Biotechnology.* www.bio.org/aboutbio/guide2000/ facts.html.

BIO (1999b) www.bio.org.

BIO (1999c) *Guide to Biotechnology,* www.bio.org/aboutbio/guide2000/ guide_health.html.

BioCommerce Data Ltd (2000) *The U.K. Biotechnology Handbook, 2000.* UK: BioCommerce Data Ltd.

Blair M (1995) *Ownership and Control – Rethinking Corporate Governance for the 21st Century.* Washington DC: The Brookings Institution.

British Embassy in Germany (2000) Personal communication, March.

British Technology Group (2000) www.btgplc.com.

Burrill & Company (1999) *Biotech 99 – Life Sciences into the Millennium.* San Francisco: Burrill & Company LLC.

Bundesverband Deutscher Kapitalbeteiligungsgesellschaften (BVK) (1994-1998) *Venture Capital in Europa.* BVK Nachrichten Special Report.

Bundesverband Deutscher Kapitalbeteiligungsgesellschaften (BVK) (1999a) *Venture Capital in den USA 1998.* Special Report, July 15.

Bundesverband Deutscher Kapitalbeteiligungsgesellschaften (BVK) (1999b) *Venture Capital in Europa 1998.* Special Report, July 9.

Carlin W and Soskice D (1997) 'Shocks to the system: the German political economy under stress.' *National Institute Economic Review,* No. 159: 57-66.

Charkham J (1995) *Keeping Good Company: A Study of Corporate Governance in Five Countries.* Oxford: Oxford University Press.

Clement M (2000) Personal communication, May.

CMR International (1999) *The Pharmaceutical R&D Compendium 1999 Edition.* Surrey: CMR International and PJB Publications Ltd.

CMR International (2000) *CMR International News, Spring 2000.* Vol. 18; No. 1; Surrey: CMR International.

Cooke P (1999) *Biotechnology Clusters in the UK: Lessons from Localisation in the Commercialisation of Science.* Centre for Advanced Studies, Cardiff University, Cardiff.

Curnock-Cook J (1999) Personal communication.

Dechema (2000). Informationsekretariat Biotechnologie (ISB) www.Dechema.de/deutsch/isb/firmen/kpharm.htm.

Deutsche Bank Research (1999) *German Biotech – New Star in the Universe.* Deutsche Bank Research German Equities Biotechnology Group, April 27.

Deutsche Bundesbank (1998) *Monthly Report.* April.

Dewhurst M, Hazlewood J, Holcomb M, Murphy M and Pinkus G (1999) 'Licensing and alliances – strategic tools for biotechs', in *Building for Value from Discovery to Launch.* McKinsey & Company, 65-74.

DiMasi JD, Hansen R, Grabowski HG and Lasagna L (1991) 'Cost of innovation in the pharmaceutical industry.' *Journal of Health Economics,* No. 10: 107-142.

Dore R (1985) 'Structures and the long term view.' *Policy Studies,* Vol. 6, Part 1, July, 10-28.

Dore R, Lazonick W and O'Sullivan M (1999) 'Varieties of capitalism in the twentieth century.' *Oxford Review of Economic Policy,* Vol. 15, No. 4, 102-120.

DTI (1999) *Genome Valley Report – The Economic Potential and Strategic Importance of Biotechnology in the UK.* London: Department of Trade and Industry.

DTI/British Embassy in Germany (1998) *Biotechnology in Germany – Report of an ITS Expert Mission.* Bonn: British Embassy.

E*Trade (2000) www.etrade.com, May.

(The) Economist (1997) January 25, 16.

108   *(The) Economist* (1998) 'Management shortfall.' July 18.

Edwards J and Fischer K (1994) *Banks, Finance and Investment in Germany.* Cambridge: Cambridge University Press.

Ernst & Young (1998a) *Biotech 99: Bridging the Gap – 13th Biotechnology Industry Annual Report.* California: Ernst & Young LLP.

Ernst & Young (1998b) *New Directions 1998 – 12th Biotechnology Industry Annual Report.* California: Ernst & Young LLP.

Ernst & Young (1998c) *European Life Sciences 98 – Continental Shift.* London: Ernst & Young International.

Ernst & Young (1999) *European Life Sciences 99 – Communicating Value.* London: Ernst & Young International.

Ernst & Young (2000) *European Life Sciences 2000 – Evolution.* London: Ernst & Young International.

European Private Equity and Venture Capital Association (EVCA) *Yearbooks* 1993-1998.

Florida R and Kenney M (1986) 'Venture capital – financial innovation and technological change in the USA.' *Research Policy*, Vol. 17, 119-137.

Genome Pharmaceuticals Corporation (2000) www.gpc-ag.com.

Hemington Scott (2000) www.hemingtonscott.com, May.

Henderson R, Orsenigo L and Pisano G (1998) 'The Pharmaceutical Industry and the Revolution in Molecular Biology: Exploring the Interactions between Scientific, Institutional and Organizational Change.' Draft, written for the CCC Matrix Project.

Hollingsworth R (1997) 'Continuities and changes in social systems of production: the cases of Germany, Japan, and the United States', in Hollingsworth R and Boyer R, eds. *Contemporary Capitalism.* Cambridge: Cambridge University Press.

Katzenstein P (1987) *Policy and Politics in West Germany: towards the Growth of a Semisovereign State.* Philadelphia: Temple University Press.

Katzenstein P (1989) 'Stability and change in the emerging Third Republic', in Katzenstein P, ed. *Industry and Politics in West Germany.* Ithica: Cornell University Press.

Kenney M (1986) 'Schumpeterian innovation and entrepreneurs in capitalism: a case study of the U.S. biotechnology industry.' *Research Policy*, Vol. 15, 21-31.

Kettler H (1997) 'Transitions to Competitiveness: Problems of Economic Restructuring in East Germany.' PhD dissertation, University of Notre Dame, Notre Dame, IN.

Kettler H (1999) *Updating the Cost of a New Chemical Entity*. London: Office of Health Economics.

Khanna T, Gulati R and Nohria N (1998) 'The dynamics of learning alliances: competition, cooperation, and relative scope.' *Strategic Management Journal*, Vol. 19, 193-210.

Lehman Brothers (2000) 'Oxford GlycoSciences plc.' Report, 25 February; London: Lehman Brothers.

Lehrer M (1997) 'German industrial strategy in turbulence: corporate governance and managerial hierarchies in Lufthansa.' *Industry and Innovation*, 4, 115-140.

Lerner J and Merges R (1998) 'The control of technology alliances: an empirical analysis of the biotechnology industry.' *The Journal of Industrial Economics*, Vol. XLVI, June, 125-156.

Lerner J and Tsai A (1999) 'Financing R&D through Alliances: Contract Structure and Outcomes in Biotechnology.' Draft of a working paper.

Macalister T (2000) 'Biotech sector finds new life.' *The Guardian*, January 19, 27.

Mackewicz and Partner (1998) *Venture Capital and Corporate Venture Capital: Financing Alternatives for Innovative Start-ups and Young Technology Companies in Germany*. Munich: Mackewicz and Partner.

Max Planck Society (1999) www.mpg.de.

McKinsey and Company (1998) *US Venture Capital – Industry Overview and Economics*. McKinsey and Company, September.

Merrill Lynch (1999) *Biotechnology Product Pipelines*. April 8.

Merrill Lynch (2000) *Biotechnology March Model Handbook*. March 20.

Mietsch A (1999) *Bio-Technologie – Das Jahr- und Adressbuch 1999*. Berlin: BIOCOM.

110   Milgrom P and Roberts J (1992) *Economics, Organization, and Management.* Eaglewood Cliffs: Prentice Hill.

Miller G (1992) *Managerial Dilemmas.* Cambridge: Cambridge University Press.

Momma S and Sharp M (1999) 'Developments in new biotechnology firms in Germany.' *Technovation,* Vol. 19, 267-282.

Monks R and Minow N (1995) *Corporate Governance.* London: Blackwell.

National Institutes of Health (NIH) (2000) www.grants.nih.gov, May.

Nelson R (1999) *Sources of Industrial Leadership: Studies of Seven Industries.* Cambridge: Cambridge University Press.

Oakey R, Faulkner W, Cooper S and Walsh V (1990) *New Firms in the Biotechnology Industry.* London: Pinter.

Office of Technology Policy (1997) *Meeting the Challenge: US Industry Faces the 21st Century – The U.S. Biotechnology Industry.* US Department of Commerce.

Olsen & Associates (2000) www.oanda.com.

Penan H (1996) 'R&D strategy in a techno-economic network: Alzheimer's disease therapeutic strategies.' *Research Policy,* Vol. 25, 337-358.

Platika D (1999) 'Checking out of the Roach Motel, or how to keep from checking in.' *Nature Biotechnology,* Vol. 17, Supplement, BE3-BE6.

Powell W (1996) 'Inter-organizational collaboration in the biotechnology industry.' *Journal of Institutional and Theoretical Economics,* Vol. 152, No. 1, 197-215.

Powell W (1999) 'The social construction of an organizational field: the case of biotechnology.' *International Journal of Biotechnology,* Vol. 1, No. 1, 42-66.

Powell W and Brantley P (1994) 'Competitive cooperation in biotechnology: learning through networks?' in Nohria N and Eccles R, eds. *Networks and Organisations: Structure, Form and Action.* Boston: Harvard Business School Press, 311-347.

Powell W, Koput K and Smith-Doerr L (1996) 'Interorganizational collaboration and the locus of innovation: networks of learning in biotechnology.' *Administrative Science Quarterly*, Vol. 41, 116-145.

Recombinant Capital (2000) www.recap.com.

Romanowski G (1999) 'Biotechnology in Germany.' *Journal of Commercial Biotechnology*, Vol. 6, No. 1, Summer, 20-24.

Sainsbury et al. (1999) *Biotechnology Clusters*, Report of Mission for Minister of Science, London, August.

Saxenian A (1994) *Regional Advantage*. Cambridge: Harvard University Press.

Schitag Ernst & Young (1998) *Germany's Biotechnology Takes Off in 1998*. Stuttgart: Schitag Ernst & Young.

Schmoch U (1999) 'Interaction of universities and industrial enterprises in Germany and the United States – a comparison.' *Industry and Innovation*, Vol. 6, No. 1.

Science Watch (1992) 'A ranking of university institutes by citation impact: current contents: life sciences. Molecular biology/genetics subsection.' Philadelphia: Institute of Scientific Information.

Senker J (1996) 'National systems of innovation, organizational learning and industrial biotechnology.' *Technovation*, Vol. 16, No. 5, 219-229.

SG Cowen (1998) 'Biotechnology in Europe - A road map for investors with lessons from America.' *Perspectives*, September.

SG Cowen (2000a) 'Global biotechnology quarterly.' *Perspectives*, March.

SG Cowen (2000b) 'European biotechnology – short-term volatility, long-term appreciation.' *Quarterly*, March.

Sharp M (1999) 'The science of nations: European multinationals and American biotechnology.' *International Journal of Biotechnology*, Vol. 1, No. 1, 132-162.

Silvia S (1999) *Reversal of Fortune? An Assessment of the German Biotechnology Sector in Comparative Perspective*. Economic Studies Program Series Volume 5: The John Hopkins University.

111

112 Simpson H (1998) *Biotechnology and the Economics of Discovery in the Pharmaceutical Industry.* London: Office of Health Economics.

Soskice D (1997) 'German technology policy, innovation, and national institutional frameworks.' *Industry and Innovation,* 4: 75-96.

Streeck W (1984) *Industrial Relations in West Germany: A Case Study of the Car Industry.* New York: St. Martin's Press.

Stuart T (1999) *Interorganizational Alliances and the Performance of Firms: A Study of Growth and Innovation Rates in a High-Technology Industry.* Working Paper, Graduate School of Business, University of Chicago.

tbg (1999) Personal communication, March.

tbg (2000) Personal communication, March.

Towse A and Leighton T (1999) 'The changing nature of NCE pricing of second and subsequent entrants', in Sussex J and Marchant N, eds. *Risk and Return in the Pharmaceutical Industry.* London: Office of Health Economics, 91-106.

Tylecote A and Conesa E (1999) 'Corporate governance, innovation systems, and industrial policy.' *Industry and Innovation* 6, 25-50.

Vitols S, Casper S, Soskice D and Wolcook S (1997) *Corporate Governance in Large British and Germany Companies.* London: Anglo-German Foundation.

Warburg Dillon Read (2000a) *At a Crossroads.* London: Warburg Dillon Read Global Equity Research Europe, February.

Warburg Dillon Read (2000b) *Biotechnology Sector Update – Rolling Thunder.* London: Warburg Dillon Read Global Equity Research Europe, March 10.

Warburg Dillon Read (2000c) *Biotechnology Sector Update – The Blair Genome Project.* London: Warburg Dillon Read Global Equity Research Europe, March 16.

Werth B (1994) *The Billion-Dollar Molecule.* New York: Touchstone, Simon & Schuster.

Windhover Information Inc (2000) *Pharmaceutical Strategic Alliances.*

Wirtschaftswoche (2000) 'Aktien statt Mitbestimmung.' March 9, pp. 178-179.

REFERENCES

Zucker L and Darby M (1999) 'Star scientist linkages to firms in APEC   **113**
and European countries: indicators of regional institutional differences
affecting competitive advantage.' *International Journal of Biotechnology*,
Vol. 1, No. 1, 119-131.

Zucker L, Darby M and Armstrong J (1994) 'Intellectual human capital
and the firm: the technology of geographically localized spillovers.'
Economic Inquiry, Jan., 36 (1), 65-86.

Zucker L, Darby M and Brewer M (1998) 'Intellectual human capital and
the birth of US biotechnology enterprises.' *American Economic Review*,
March, 88(1): 290-306.

APPENDIX 1 – EXCHANGE RATE TABLE

114

1€ =	1994	1995	1996	1997	1998	1999
UK£	0.7833	0.8266	0.7363	0.6638	0.6986	0.6232
US$	1.2254	1.2808	1.2395	1.1128	1.1726	1.0068
DM	1.8998	1.8360	1.9285	1.9781	1.9632	1.9558

Note: Rates are for the end of December each year.

Source: Olsen & Associates (2000).

APPENDIX 2 - CONTRIBUTORS

Interviews in Germany:
Professor Dr. Ulrich Abshagen, Heidelberg Innovation GmbH
Anthony Arke, EuropaBio
Dr. Bernhard Arnolds, BioValley The Life Sciences Net Works
E. Fritshi, PhD, BioGenTec
Dr. Jens Fuerste, Noxxon Pharma AG
Dr. Ernst-Dieter Jarasch, BioRegion Rein-Neckar-Dreieck e.V.
Dr. Frieder Kern, Deutsches Krebsforschungszentrum
Dr. Rainer Kuehn, Boehringer Mannheim GmbH
Dr. Monika Matthes, Industrial Investment Council, The New
German Länder
Dr. Thomas Meier, MyoContract
Ron Meyer, Newlab Diagnostic Systems GmbH
Joerg Poetzsch, PhD, Atugen AG
Prof. Dr. Peter Stadler, Artemis Pharmaceuticals GmbH.
Corinna Wernet, BioGenTec

Interviews in the UK:
Colin Bain, Magdalen Science Park
Professor Baker, BBSRC
J. Benjamin, Advent
Joe Carey, Technology Transfer Office, University of Sussex
Mark Clement, Merlin Biosciences
Jeremy Curnock Cook, Rothschild Asset Management Ltd.
Monica Darnbrough, DTI
Dr. Janet Dewdney, Adprotech
David Ellis, Euromedica
Dr. Chris Evans, Merlin Biosciences
Dr. Finer, CIA
Dr. Jonathan Hepple, Rothschild Asset Management Ltd.
Dr. Trevor Jones, ABPI
Dr. Melanie Lee, Celltech
Robert Mansfield, Vanguard Medica
Peter McDonald, DTI
Dr. Riddel, Pharmagene
John Sime, BIA

116 Christine Soden, Chiroscience
Edward Wawrzynczak, Rothschild Asset Management Ltd.

Interviews in the US:
Dr. Karen Cockley, Michael O'Niell, and Tony Crowe, Wyeth-Ayerst
Dr. Martha Connolley, MD Department of Business and Economic
Development
Duc Duong, High Technology Council of MD
Chad Evans, Council on Competitiveness
Chuck Ludlam, BIO
Philip Ufholz, BIO
Debra van Opstal, Council on Competitiveness
Gillian Woollett, PhRMA
Dr. Stephen Yoder, Pfizer

Institutions that contributed information:
Arthur Andersen, Life Sciences Group, Cambridge UK
British Embassy, Bonn, Germany
Bundesverband Deutscher Kapitalbeteiligungsgesellschaften (BVK),
Berlin Germany
Dechema – Informationsekretariat Biotechnologie, Frankfurt
Germany
Ernst & Young, Life Sciences Industry Group, Cambridge UK
Warburg Dillon Read (now UBS Warburg), London UK
Windhover Information Inc., South Norwalk, CT, US

RECENT OHE PUBLICATIONS

Managing to do Better: General Practice in the 21st Century
by Gordon Moore, 2000 (price £7.50)

Prices, Competition and Regulation in Pharmaceuticals: a Cross-national Comparison
by Patricia Danzon and Li-Wei Chao, 2000 (price £10.00)

Benchmarking and Incentives in the NHS
by Paul Grout, Andrew Jenkins and Carol Propper, 2000 (price £7.50)

Primary Care and the NHS Reforms: a Manager's View
by Robert Royce, 2000 (price £10.00)

Narrowing the Gap between Provision and Need for Medicines in Developing Countries
by Hannah Kettler, 2000 (price £7.50)

Risk Adjusting Health Care Resource Allocations – Theory and Practice in the UK,
The Netherlands and Germany
by Adam Oliver, 1999 (price £7.50)

Genomics, Healthcare and Public Policy
eds. Paul Williams and Sarah Clow, 1999 (price £10.00)

Doctors, Economics and Clinical Practice Guidelines: Can they be Brought Together?
by David Eddy, 1999 (price £5.00)

Leadership, Change and Primary Care Groups
ed. Louise Locock, 1999 (price £5.00)

Public Involvement in Priority Setting
ed. Lisa Gold, 1999 (price £5.00)

Risk and Return in the Pharmaceutical Industry
eds. Jon Sussex and Nick Marchant, 1999 (price £10.00)

The New NHS: What Can We Learn from Managed Care in New Zealand and the US?
ed. Nick Goodwin, 1999 (price £5.00)

Trade Mark Legislation and the Pharmaceutical Industry
by Shelley Lane with Jeremy Phillips, 1999 (price £10.00)

Organisational Costs in the New NHS
by Bronwyn Croxson, 1999 (price £7.50)

Disease Management, the NHS and the Pharmaceutical Industry
by Anne Mason, Adrian Towse and Mike Drummond, 1999 (price £7.50)

Updating the Cost of a New Chemical Entity
by Hannah Kettler, 1999 (price £7.50)